My Life, M[...] My Kurdistan

CHIMAN ZEBARI

Copyright © 2015 by Chiman Zebari. 704998
Edited by Benjamin Kweskin
Photography by Carol Griffith-Roberts of Precious Posh Photography

Library of Congress Control Number: 2015908325
ISBN: Softcover   978-1-5035-7305-5
         Hardcover   978-1-5035-7304-8
         EBook   978-1-5035-7306-2

This is a work of fiction. Names, characters,
places and incidents either are the product of the
author's imagination or are used fictitiously, and any
resemblance to any actual persons, living or dead,
events, or locales is entirely coincidental.

Print information available on the last page

Rev. date: 06/16/2015

To order additional copies of this book, contact:
Xlibris
1-888-795-4274
www.Xlibris.com
Orders@Xlibris.com

My Life, My Food, My Kurdistan

CHIMAN ZEBARI

CONTENTS

Preface

It was a forced vulnerability, I like to say. These emotions did not just include helplessness but also the heavy hand of human vengeance. Men and women alike displayed extraordinary courage in coping with the bombings, but our conditions were forced by the political powers of the day. This is where Ingrid's story intersects my story because she too experienced this forced vulnerability in her active duty service. Like me, opposing enemies (or the powers that be) imposed our vulnerability and determined who lived, who died, who mattered, and who didn't. In these terrible and fraught moments, I wondered: Is it my day to die? Do I matter?

These events happened to me as a child and I did not grasp the mortality of the moment. Ingrid, on the other hand, was already a woman, a mother, and a soldier who left a child behind for service to the nation. I know that she was afraid that she would never see her daughter again. This forced vulnerability often manifests itself as a sunken feeling, not for fear of death, but rather what will happen to people that we leave behind—children, spouses, parents, or other loved ones. This is my story, about how I fled my home and ultimately wound up in the United States with my husband and children.

Foreword

by Ingrid A. Parker

 My Life, My Food, My Kurdistan is a compelling story of a woman who immigrated to the United States after Saddam Hussein's tyranny and purging of the Kurds in the 1970s. As a young girl, Chiman was in an arranged marriage, yet ultimately, she tells a story of personal strength, achievement, and autonomy. She shows us that even the most turbulent journeys are often simultaneously rewarding. I would like to take this moment to acknowledge this powerful story from a strong woman and good friend.

 My name is Ingrid Parker, and I assisted with the editing of this cookbook with Chiman Zebari. I am writing in Chiman's cookbook because I think that we are kindred spirits, both on life journeys that brought us together by circumstance and opportunity. I like to think our journeys were voyages that women were not supposed to or allowed to take, but we took those journeys anyway. Our journeys allowed us to achieve a surprising autonomy in our lives, careers, and personal choices. Even today, we continue to follow similar paths. Our shared journey is perhaps more purposeful today than in the past as we are friends and continue to develop our friendship. I am a lieutenant colonel in the United States Army who is working on a PhD in the Language, Literacy, and Culture program at the University of Baltimore County. My dissertation topic fortuitously led to my interest and eventual friendship with Chiman. This topic stems from a deployment to Baghdad Province with the First Advise and Assist Brigade, Third Infantry Division, in 2009 when I still had the rank of major.

At the time, I was the executive officer for one of the battalions in the brigade, called the Brigade Special Troops Battalion. Our battalion was responsible for managing Forward Operating Base Falcon in terms of security and the contractual obligations that operated the base. During the course of operations and daily work, I began to meet and interact with Iraqi women who, unbeknownst to most, were rebuilding Iraq alongside the Iraqi men. These women were very committed to improving Iraq and their communities. These women were contractors, teachers, lawyers, nongovernment organizational leaders, and businesswomen. It was during this time that I became interested in the lives of these women. Prior to these chance encounters, I had preconceptions about Muslim women—probably garnered from newscasts or other half-truths. As I reflect on meeting these women, I am aware that we were brought together mostly by chance; however, I personally wanted to pay it forward in some meaningful way. By *paying it forward*, I mean that I wanted to improve circumstances for people in Iraq rather than only contributing to the forces of war. At that time, I did not know how I was going to do that, but I knew that I would jump in if the opportunity presented itself. Over time, an opportunity did arise. It first started with the chance meetings of several women that led us to plan and conduct a large Iraqi women's conference in Baghdad. Upon leaving Baghdad, the Iraqi women I had befriended were concerned that I would forget them. I told them I would not and could not discard all that we tried to do. In the end, the best way to illuminating the strides of Iraqi women is to tell their stories. I plan to write these stories as part of my dissertation, and I hope to bring awareness to the situation for women in Iraq, both good and bad.

When I met Chiman, it was my third (maybe fourth) accidental meeting with Iraqi women. This time, my life intersected her life in the United States. She is a Kurdish American woman who lives in Northern Virginia. Because I was scheduled to attend the Regional Oral History Office's annual conference at the University of Berkeley in 2012, I wanted to practice oral history interviewing prior to the conference. Someone at work mentioned that I might want to talk to Chiman as she was very active in Iraqi politics and the issues of Iraqi women. Therefore, I called her immediately. When I first called Chiman, I really thought we would meet and work together just for my summer project; however, since that time, we have become good friends, and she continues to be part of my life and dissertation work.

When I contacted Chiman Zebari for an interview, it was to practice the in-depth interview, the methodology for dissertation. For both of us, it was a serendipitous occurrence. Because the art of interviewing is in the mastery of question-asking, Chiman was the perfect interviewee because she spoke English and was very articulate. For my purposes, I needed to find someone who understood the topics that I planned to write about—women's marginalization in Iraq and the United States (US) Army. That said, I was completely unaware of how rich Chiman's experiences were until I interviewed her. Like me, she was interested in the manner in which Iraqi-Muslim women were represented in the West, in American politics, and in academia. Both of us found the Western representations of Iraqi women inaccurate and one-sided. Sure, life "is and was" harsh for Iraqi women; however, that is not the whole story. And there is something important in telling the whole story.

Because we come from different backgrounds and upbringings, I often asked questions, framing them in a Western way. Therefore, I had to learn how to (re)frame questions for different and Muslim women audience. This is something that requires practice, so Chiman's interviews were valuable lessons in designing the questions, and I appreciated her time and patience with me. Chiman also brought an amazing résumé—not just a work résumé, but a family résumé too as she married into the Zebari clan, a political family in Iraq. The Zebaris are a powerful political family in Iraq and Kurdistan and have been involved in politics for many years. These family connections afford her powerful insight into the political activities in both Iraq and Kurdistan.

As you read, both Chiman and I believe in storytelling and in women-for-women empowerment, a theme we use in this cookbook. We posit that much of our American identity is politically constructed—meaning it is real but at the expense of other women and, in this case, Iraqi women. It is true that we are successful women by Western standards; however, the triple paradox (gender, race, and class or gender, religion, and class) renders an invisibility on subjects that feel real too (DuBois 1903, 5). With statement, we recognize our own marginalization and opt *not* to (re)invent East-West binaries for other women by acknowledging one's personal journeys and bringing the plurality of women's voices into history.

From my perspective, I think people come into our lives to teach us something that we did not know or could not see due to social construction and the invisibility that it creates. This invisibility is purposeful and by design; however, its transparency maintains one's social placement and keeps us blind to the plight of others. Consequently, we understand the world through our own experiences and our social constructs, but perhaps, some lessons come in other ways—through chance meetings with people of other cultures. Now in my late forties, I wonder if those meetings are chance at all or rather cues from something greater than the self.

Chapter 1

My Story

My name is Chiman Zebari and I would like to share with you the history of my people—the Kurdish people—and to share my own story: how I came to be a refugee in the United States, my family background, and also importantly, share several tasty Kurdish recipes! I have always wanted to write the history of my life, but I hesitated for a while because the task of writing an autobiography is quite complicated, emotional, and difficult.

I will begin by telling the story about my birthplace, Aqrah (or Akrê). The people living in Aqrah are mostly Kurds and are the indigenous Kurdish Bahdini (Kurmanji) speakers from the Bahdinan region, which is part of northwestern Iraqi Kurdistan, or officially known as the Kurdistan Region of Iraq, or what we call Southern Kurdistan. Bahdinan covers the cities of Amediye, Aqrah, Dohuk, Sinjar, and Zakho. Aqrah is a beautiful and ancient city developed in a steep hillside above a thriving old market, located about twenty-four kilometers south of the famous village of Barzan. It is northeast of Erbil (Kurdish: Hewler) by approximately two hours. Aqrah once had a large Christian and Jewish population. The population of

Photograph by Carol Griffith-Roberts of Precious Posh Photography

Aqrah is in the tens of thousands and made up of Kurds and Assyrian Christians living together peacefully. The winter in Aqrah is extremely cold and the summer is hot, but the spring and fall are gorgeous and indescribable. The mountains are covered in green grass and wildflowers in the springtime. When you look from far away, you'll think it is a green blanket covering the mountain. Though the area is full of natural beauty and history spanning thousands of years, the people are singularly the best thing about this region.

Introduction to Kurds

This book is intended for readers who are not familiar with the Kurds and Kurdistan who would like to learn about Kurdish culture and history. I hope this book will offer a broad perspective regarding the importance of family values in Kurdish culture and how it is being preserved by Kurds who live in Western countries. I am not writing this book from the viewpoint of every Kurdish woman but, rather, based on my personal experiences as a Kurdish-American woman—someone who has experienced life in Kurdish society as well as in American society.

In this section, I would like to introduce the Kurdish people in general and my family in particular. The Kurds are an ancient people with ancient ties to their land. The Kurds have been pulled and displaced from their homeland for centuries. The Kurdish homeland is called Kurdistan, which is divided between Turkey, Syria, Iraq, and Iran. Kurdistan is often referred to as one of those "Alice in Wonderland"-type countries that do not officially exist. However, it does in fact exist and lies in the heart of the Middle East, contrary to the denial of its neighboring countries.

According to the book *The Kurdish People: A People without a Homeland*, Kurds "are the largest ethnic group in the world without a country of their own." Kurds have been punished not only for their political views but also for cultural and language differences; furthermore, they have often been persecuted and punished for their religious and political beliefs. Kurds are a loving and peaceful people and accept and respect all other religions equally.

One of the most ancient religions practiced by the Kurds prior to Islam, as well as today, is Zoroastrianism. Though most eventually converted to Islam, a small minority have remained Zoroastrian while others still follow Yezidism, Judaism, and Christianity. In addition, there are other religions, such as Kakayee (also called Ahl-al-Haq and Yarsan), which is similar to the Druze religion. It is believed that the followers (of Kakayee) have the same beliefs as the Zoroastrians.

Today, Islam is the dominant religion in Kurdistan, and each year, thousands of Muslim Kurds go on a pilgrimage called hajj. The Muslims gather in Mecca, Saudi Arabia, for the annual event, which is the largest religious gathering among Muslims in the world. In Islam, the pilgrimage is a duty upon every Muslim adult physically and financially capable to make the journey. Hajj is one of the five pillars of the faith, which they celebrate for the glory of God (Allah).

The Jews are one of the longest surviving groups in Iraq and they are primarily the result of the Assyrian and Babylonian exiles in 734 BCE and 597 BCE, respectively. In my birthplace, Aqrah, there were many Jews who lived there; however, the Iraqi government killed many of them and forced virtually the entire community to Israel by 1952. These people were forcibly evicted after the Israeli War of Independence in 1948 when things changed in Iraq (and in the rest of the Arab world as well). Some Jews chose to convert to Islam, at least officially, so they could stay in their homes. Many of the converted Jews married Muslims, and some descendants are yet unaware of their ancestors' decisions.

Chapter 2

Brief Kurdish Conflict and Political Parties

It is difficult to understand the Kurds and their ongoing conflicts with their neighboring countries unless you have a basic knowledge of key chronological events in their history. For purposes of my story and how the struggle of the Kurds led my family and myself to the United States, I will provide a brief snapshot of these events up to the mid-1970s. One can quickly get caught up to speed on the key events in Kurdish history with some base time frame. In 1918, during World War I, the Ottoman Empire collapsed and British forces occupied the oil-rich Ottoman province of Mosul, the second largest city in modern-day Iraq. This occupation also included nearly all majority Kurdish-populated areas. Sheikh Mahmud Barzinji revolted against this forced colonial British rule and declared a Kurdish kingdom in parts of Southern Kurdistan (northern Iraq). In 1920, the Treaty of Sevres was signed by the defeated Ottoman government which included a provision in support of the establishment of an independent Kurdish state, subject to a subsequent agreement by the League of Nations. In article 64 of this treaty, the Kurds were granted the option of joining a future Kurdish state. However, in 1923, Kemal Ataturk gained international recognition for his newly formed "secular" Republic of Turkey with the signing of the Treaty of Lausanne since the previously signed Sevres Treaty was not ratified by the Turkish Parliament. In 1932, uprisings began in the Barzan region, protesting the admittance of Iraq into the League of Nations, while the Kurds' demands for autonomy were completely ignored. The late leader Mullah Mustafa Barzani led another uprising in 1943, which resulted in controlling large areas, including Erbil and the Bahdinan region of Southern Kurdistan.

Central to these political struggles in the modern era are several political parties. The Kurdistan Democratic Party (KDP) is a political party founded in 1946 and was led by Mullah Mustafa Barzani for over fifty years. In this same year as the establishment of the KDP, the first independent state was founded by Qazi Muhammad in Mahabad, Iran, also referred to as the Mahabad Republic. Unfortunately, the Mahabad Republic collapsed within less than one full year due to attacks from Iranian forces. President Qazi Muhammad was hanged by the Iranian government for his "treason." Mullah Mustafa Barzani, along with many followers, fled to the Soviet Union in 1947.

In 1951, a new generation of Kurdish nationalists revived the KDP in Iraq. Seven years later, an overthrow of the Iraqi monarchy allowed Kurdish nationalists to organize openly, and a new Iraqi constitution recognized Kurdish "national rights." Mullah Mustafa Barzani returned from exile that same year. Two short years later, relations between the Iraqi government and Kurdish groups started to become tense and the KDP was dissolved by the Iraqi government after another Kurdish rebellion.

The 1970s proved to be a trying decade for the Kurds. In March 1970, the Iraqi government and the Kurdish parties agreed to a peace accord, which again granted the Kurds a level of autonomy. This accord was supposedly going to recognize Kurdish as an official language in Iraq and an amendment in the Iraqi constitution was to include the wording: "The Iraqi . . . is made up of two nationalities, the Arab nationality and the Kurdish nationality." Just a year later, however, relations between the Kurds and the Iraqi government deteriorated once more, and Mullah Mustafa Barzani appealed to the United States for aid for the Kurdish struggle.

Ultimately, this peace plan failed and erupted into the Second Kurdish-Iraqi War, which escalated the Kurdish-Iraqi conflict. At this time, the Iraqi dictator Saddam Hussein issued a warrant to arrest all Kurdish men who were actively supporting the Kurdish cause; many people secretly escaped the country. Some were lucky to take their families with them, while others had to escape alone and leave their families behind. In mid-1974, my father and his brother left Erbil and escaped to Choman, a Kurdish town near the Iranian border, where they served as *Peshmerga*. My mother, siblings, aunt, and cousins were all left behind, and we did not hear from my father for several months.

My family are considered Iraqis in the eyes of the international community. However, we do not consider ourselves Iraqi but Kurds. We have our own identity, culture, food, language, values, and so on. My father was a member of the KDP; he served as a *Peshmerga* freedom fighter (literally, those who face death) and fought against the brutal Iraqi regime. During that time, all Kurdish political activities were underground because if they were caught, they would have been persecuted and even worse.

Chapter 3

My Family Story

In the past, when a Kurdish man got married, he lived with his extended family. When my mother got married, she lived at the same house as my grandfather, grandmother, three uncles, their wives, and children. The house was huge, and each couple had their own private room, but they would share the rest of the house. They all cooked and ate together; they were one family.

My grandfather was a wealthy merchant and had several stores in Aqrah. He himself was a member of the KDP and was secretly aiding the *Peshmerga*, who would travel through the town with food and necessities. My grandfather had four sons and three daughters. One of his sons, along with my father, worked with him and helped him take care of the family business. My younger uncle, Mohammad, was teaching at a school in southern Iraq, but he would come home for the weekends, which back then was considered Thursdays and Fridays. On Fridays, the majority of the men go to the mosque for the Friday prayers while the women pray at home.

In the late 1960s, I vaguely remember I was once playing with my cousins in our beautiful orchard when I heard gunshots. My cousins and I wanted to go up on the roof to see where they were coming from. We thought that a couple had gotten married and they were shooting in the air to celebrate. In the Middle East, it is normal to shoot in the air when someone gets married since it is considered a symbol of happiness and make loud noise like fireworks. Nevertheless, not long after that, we heard the shooting getting closer and closer. After a few minutes, I saw a group of armed men smashing things with the butts of their rifles and throwing gasoline on everything. It was not until later we found out that some of the Zebari family had previously joined the Ba'ath Party (the party of Saddam Hussein) and collaborated with the Iraqi government against their own people.

My parents in Nashville TN, 1988.

All families have good people and bad people. After this incident, the relations between the Barzanis and Zebaris became somewhat strained, and in order to strengthen relations among the two tribes again, they had to marry within the tribes. It is worth noting that the late Gen. Mustafa Barzani's second wife is the daughter of Mahmud Agha Zebari, a well-known Zebari family member. She was the sister of the current Iraqi foreign minister, Mr. Hoshyar Zebari, and the mother of the current president, Masoud Barzani. Mullah Mustafa's older brother, Sheikh Ahmad Barzani, also was married to a woman from the Zebari clan.

In order to make the readers understand and follow who's who, it is important to know the history to some degree. Sheikh Ahmad Barzani was the son of Sheikh Mohammad Barzani. Sheikh Ahmad Barzani was the older brother of the late Mullah Mustafa Barzani and uncle of the current president of the Kurdistan region, Masoud Barzani.

The village of Barzan lies on the edges of Mount Shirin, and this village was multicultural and multilingual as there was once a large Assyrian and Jewish population as well as Muslim. The village of Barzan was similar to a large family, as everyone knew each other and they all took part in social events such as weddings and funerals.

My father used to speak of Sheikh Ahmed Barzani often. He said that Barzani was a peaceful man and had an easygoing personality. He never feared facing challenges head-on and was a very spiritual and religious man. Of course, he was very sympathetic to the Kurdish political movements; therefore, he became the central focus of Iraqi, Turkish, and the British discontent. Sheikh Ahmed Barzani received many Northern Kurds (modern-day Turkey) who were seeking sanctuary in the village of Barzan, where my family was living between 1968 and 1970. It was also said that Sheikh Ahmed was very humble when dealing with people and was highly respectful of the people around him regardless of their faith. Sheikh Ahmed believed people should discuss issues, and he was against the use of force unless there was no other option; he was the symbol of unity among the Barzanis. It is impossible to understand the Kurdish movement and the Barzanis' rule without the mention of Sheikh Ahmad, who was born in 1896 in Barzan and died in 1969.When Sheikh Ahmad Barzani heard about my family's tragedy, he sent for my family to come to live in Barzan until things calmed down. So we lived in Barzan for two years, and in 1970, Saddam Hussein announced an amnesty for those Kurds who had escaped; my family was included. But this time, my father decided to go to Erbil instead of his hometown of Aqrah because he it was painful for him to relive his family's tragedy.

I am married to a man from the Zebari clan, who is a Kurdish nationalist. My husband's relatives are also important and loyal supporters of the KDP and are members of the KDP. As I mentioned before, the overwhelming majority of Zebaris opposed the Iraqi regime. Those people who collaborated with the previous Iraqi regime and fought against the Kurds and were the ones who harmed my family were not from my husband's family. In addition, some of Barzani's own family members joined the Iraqi regime and fought against their own families too. In fact, Saddam Hussein never trusted any Kurd who joined his regime, especially the Barzanis. In the end, he killed most of those Kurdish men who had collaborated with his party after using them to his advantage.

The Kurds who had collaborated with the regime are commonly called *jash*, which means "little donkeys." During the previous Iraqi regime, any Kurdish person who had collaborated with the regime against their fellow Kurds was considered a traitor. At this time, jash were anti-KDP. They publicly and vocally supported the Iraqi regime and Arab nationalism in general and frequently spoke out against the dominant Kurdish political parties. My family suffered at the hands of those who had collaborated because my grandfather was one of the leading people in Aqrah who had supported Barzani.

In 1976, Saddam Hussein suddenly became a general in the Iraqi Army. Shortly after that, he became a leading member of the Ba'ath Party as well. Saddam rapidly became powerful in the government, and unfortunately, the Iraqi president, Ahmad Hassan al-Bakir, was unable to execute his duties because he was sick and weak. Over time, Saddam Hussein was able to take on more power.

Ahmed Hassan al-Bakir was sixty-five years old when he stepped down from the presidency in July 1979, supposedly due to his health. Saddam Hussein assumed vice presidency, and in 1982, Ahmed Hassan al-Bakir died.

As I grew up, I was determined to find out from my beloved father, may God bless his soul, what caused the feud to erupt between Akrawis and Zebaris. Why did they dislike each other so much? What really triggered some of the Zebaris to be so cruel, burn and loot our homes and kill several family members, like my uncle Mohammad—he was just a schoolteacher and not even involved in politics!

In hindsight, I recognize that my parents selected a good and kind man for me, but I must say that with all that happened between my family and the Zebaris, I would not have allowed my daughter to marry into that tribe. Maybe they saw something in my husband that I could or would not be able to see due to my young age. Or maybe they saw his kind heart through all the family drama and the turbulent times. It is funny how things can be simultaneously agonizing/amazing as well as weird/wonderful. It is a lesson we all learn.

My father told me that even among the Zebaris, families were divided by political views motivated by the desire for money and power. As the old proverb states, "Money is the root of all kinds of evil." This motto is frequently proven to be true.

During a raid on my family home in Aqrah, I saw my grandmother run to her room, grab her jewelry, hide it in a sack of clothes, and then attempt to leave the house. However, I saw a Zebari man hit my grandmother with the butt of his rifle, knocked her over on her face, then took the bag. I remember vaguely one of my cousins went to check on my grandmother to see if she was okay after the man robbed her and took all her jewelry. Thank God, she was okay, and my cousin helped her leave the house.

After that, I remember one of our relatives grabbed me and took me out of the house as I saw our home was on fire, the blaze getting stronger by the minute. I was just a child. I was in shock due to all of the commotion and did not know what was going on. I could not find my mother at this time; the others and I were off in a different part of the house.

It appeared that the traitors supporting the Iraqi regime had been planning to attack my family for being KDP sympathizers. They were looking for a reason to instigate a problem, so they made up a story to make people believe two prominent families (one of which was mine) had a family quarrel with the Zebaris. However, it was very clear to everyone, including the Barzanis, that this was undoubtedly revenge on my family for supporting the KDP. Being a *Peshmerga*, my father was rarely home and always in the mountains fighting for Kurdish rights. There were no televisions, but we did have a radio, and I remember all the grown-ups always glued to the radio to hear what was happening throughout Iraq.

In the spring of 1968, my uncle Mohammad, then in his early thirties, was killed by the Zebaris. He was a tall and very handsome man, a newlywed without children. This tragic day took place on a Friday. My grandfather had asked my uncle Mohammad to cover for him and watch the family shop while he was at the mosque praying. The shop sold dry goods, fabric, and all sorts of spices.

As my father told the story of what took place on this dark Friday, he mentioned that a couple of men from the Zebari family affiliated with the Iraqi regime entered our shop. One of those men started to provoke my uncle by trying to take stuff he needed from the store with no intention of paying, like they always did, adding it to their "tab," which was never paid. When my uncle told him that he could not allow him to take anything without paying, the two exchanged harsh words. At this point, Mohammad knew something was going to happen, so he went to the back of the store, retrieved his only weapon, returned to face the two men who were calling him names and demanded that they leave. However, the two men did not leave and tried to attack him so my uncle shot one of those men. The other one ran out of the store, but my uncle knew the other man was going to get help. Soon afterward, my uncle fled before a group of Zebari men surrounded the store. Although the one Zebari that was shot had died on the spot, my uncle managed to find a nearby cave and took refuge there.

However, one of the local shepherds saw him. When the Zebaris came to the location, this shepherd accepted money in exchanged for revealing my uncle's location. The Zebaris then called Mohammad and promised that if he came out, they would not kill him; they just wanted to talk about what happened. When he came out, they put a rope around his neck and dragged him on the back of pickup truck all the way to town, showing the people of Aqrah what they were capable of doing. This grisly torment continued until his skin fell off, and he later died from such torture. They tossed his body on the street.

This was a good-enough reason for these Zebaris to carry out what they came to do in the first place, which was to kill as many men from my family as they could and to destroy our homes and devastate our family forever. While these Zebari militiamen were busy torturing Mohammad, others were looking door-to-door for other men from our family or anyone related to my family to kill them. They managed to kill seven men that day and burned and looted as many homes as they could. A few days after this tragedy, after things calmed down somewhat, my mother, along with her sisters-in-law and a few neighbors, buried those bodies properly.

My mother said that when she saw Mohammad's face, she fainted because it was so disfigured, and to this day, my mother has never gotten over this loss. Even now, she always wears black and grieves over that tragic day. I frequently reminisce about those days and how her life forever changed because of those mercenaries. Fortunately, my father, his younger brother, and my grandfather escaped without harm, each escaping in a different way for the time being.

It was only a few weeks later that we found out how they escaped. My father escaped with the help of a family friend who was also a Zebari but a Barzani loyalist, and when the news of our tragedy reached Sheikh Ahmad Barzani, he sent men to help evacuate the area and take my family and others who had suffered to a village called Bileh (bi-LEH) near the village of Barzan. Bileh had roughly one hundred homes and it was not too far from Barzani's headquarters in the village of Rêzan. We were on the way to Bileh when my father and uncle caught up with us.

Approximately twenty Akrawi families were placed in large cement buildings that were similar to military barracks and had several large rooms. I remember looking up that evening and seeing thick, dark puffy clouds forming in the huge sky. I was awestruck by the lightning and loud thunder. I was scared and crying, and my mom tried to comfort me. They told me, "Don't be afraid. This is the voice of God. He is aware of our situation, and this is one way for Him to let us know He is here for us." It was comforting to know that God was with us and that He would get us through this ordeal. It was cold, and we could not get enough blankets to keep us warm, so we all bundled up next to one another for warmth.

Bileh people are called Bilays. They are friendly, hospitable, and kinder than I can put into words. Bileh is only a few miles away from Barzan, the birthplace of the Kurdish leaders Mullah Mustafa Barzani and Sheikh Ahmad Barzani. The majority of them are members of the Barzani extended family, and the others are locals loyal to the Barzani family.

My family and other Akrawis were literally protected by order of the late Sheikh Ahmad and Mullah Mustafa Barzani, the two leaders of the Barzani tribe. Sheikh Ahmed Barzani was considered the modern founder of Barzan because he brought many different Kurdish tribes under his command and expanded the Barzan region.

During Mustafa Barzani and his followers' stay in Soviet Azerbaijan, a few followers married foreign women (blond-haired and blue-eyed); so many women from Bileh were those same women, and they spoke Kurdish with an accent.

The first morning there, after a restless sleep, my mother woke us up for the breakfast our neighbors had brought. Afterward, all the children my age gathered and walked around the building. We saw some neighborhood children walking toward us. They were nice and very friendly and asked whether we would like to see a place where they played. We agreed and went with them. We walked through Bileh, a very small village.

This small village did not even have running water, indoor plumbing, or electricity, but it was under the control of Mustafa Barzani, and there were no Iraqi officials as there are in Aqrah, so we felt safe. The local children invited us to go to see the famous river, which they excitedly described for us along the way. It turned out to be the Zab River. It was there that I learned how to swim. As is customary in the Middle East, one side of the river was for women and one side for the men. Women usually did their laundry on the banks of the river. Even so, everyone seemed happy with this arrangement. Looking back now, I wonder why they were happy with this simple life, no indoor plumbing, no washers or dryers. I remember Bileh as if it was yesterday even though I was just a child.

I remember in the early 1970s, the Iraqi regime once again attacked the Kurds, and once again, we had to evacuate our new home because Iraqi aircraft were flying overhead and had begun bombing some of the nearby villages, including Bileh. My father at this time returned to the mountains with *Peshmerga* forces to fight against the regime.

The Kurdish people were frightened for their lives, and many people were suddenly in a hurry to leave the village. I remember seeing the aircraft overhead while lying in the grass with friends. It is funny how children maintain their naïveté in the worst of all circumstances. The people of Bileh ran into their homes, shouting for us to lie down and stop playing. I was scared. I thought we were all going to die in the bombardment. My mother packed blankets, pillows, and food for our trip to the mountains to hide from the Iraqi warplanes. Bilay men started to load weapons on horses while the women were responsible for loading the food and other essentials for their families.

Due to the politics of the region, the Kurds have always been mistreated by their neighboring countries. Their suffering has never been a secret; however, the international community and neighboring countries do not speak out against the injustice—probably for fear of retribution, the fear of starting another war, or sectarian violence. It seemed as though everyone kept it quiet and swept such criminal acts under the rug as if this injustice never occurred. Kurds have a proverb: "The mountain is the only Kurdish friend." I find this passage to be very true because every time Kurds faced conflict, no one offered to help. But the mountains were always there to protect us when needed. We ran toward the mountains and hid in a valley that we called home for several days. I saw foxes and turtles for the first time. I had never known true fear, but the bombings or threat of bombings kept us somewhat paralyzed. The valley between the two mountains was very deep and secluded. It is hard to explain how I felt at night, sleeping among the wildlife.

After a few long and scary days in the mountains, it was safe enough to return to our homes in Bileh. We were told that the Iraq regime was not going to attack us anymore, so we packed up and returned home. My father came home from his *Peshmerga* duties from time to time. He used to listen to the radio to be in touch with what was going on in the world, and this allowed him to monitor what was going on with the Kurdish issues as well. He was a Kurd all the way and without a doubt a Barzani partisan.

As I remember, the news broadcast was entirely in Arabic. None of us children spoke Arabic fluently, but we managed to understand some of the newscast because we took Arabic in school. In addition, we picked up more Arabic from listening to the Arabic music and news. I even remember hearing an English word—*autonomy*—as a child, and I did not know what it meant, but I knew it was a good thing because whenever it was said, I could see elation in the faces of many of the adults.

My father had a short temper and used to get easily irritated whenever he heard something negative about the Kurds or the Barzanis on the radio broadcast. Of course, the radio stations broadcasting from Baghdad would accuse our leader, Mullah Mustafa Barzani, of Zionism and call Kurds rebels. All this media propaganda was just a way of incriminating the Kurds for not being loyal to the Ba'ath regime. Baghdad authorities were irritated with the Kurds because Kurds accepted Jews and have historically lived with them without any conflict.

While we were in Bileh, my mother gave birth to her fifth child, a boy. Now my parents had three daughters and two sons. In the same year, then Iraqi president, Ahmad Hassan al-Bakir, invited Mustafa Barzani to go to Baghdad to discuss Kurdish autonomy; however, Barzani did not accept the invitation. Instead, al-Bakir sent his then secretary-general of the Ba'ath Party, Saddam Hussein, to tell Barzani that the Kurds and Arabs would have to live in Iraq like brothers and they would give the Kurds autonomy.

In March 1970, my family, along with other Aqrawi families, were ready to leave Bileh and head home. We were all ecstatic because we were going to go back to our normal lives! All the families gathered, packed up their belongings, got into jeeps and trucks, and headed home. My family left Bileh but headed to the large city of Erbil, and my parents started to slowly rebuild their lives from scratch.

Erbil dates back at least eight thousand years. This ancient city was originally called Arba'illu, Assyrian for "four gods." This city has seen many different rulers, including the Assyrian, Sumerian, Persian, and Sassanian dynasties.

Currently, Erbil is the fourth largest city in Iraq, located roughly five hours north of Baghdad. We started to build our lives slowly and started going back to school and studied in Kurdish. However, we also took Arabic and English classes at school, which was also great. Every morning when we arrived at school, we had to line up and sing the Iraqi national anthem. Schools in Iraq were very strict. We had to wear black and white uniforms. We could not wear nail polish or jewelry.

My parents, uncle, and grandfather lived in Erbil, not far from each other. My grandfather started to rebuild his business as a merchant. One day when he went to work, while he was opening the store, an unmarked car deliberately hit my grandfather, killing him instantly. Once more, my family felt devastated and vulnerable. We never found out exactly who killed him. We assumed it was a member of the Ba'ath Party or sympathizers.

Soon after their empty promise of providing Kurdish autonomy, the Iraqi regime started an Arabization program in the oil-rich regions in Kirkuk and Khanaqin in order to nationalize Iraq's oil industry. Mullah Mustafa Barzani was an intelligent man. He knew not to believe the empty promises of the Iraqi government from the beginning. As predicted by Barzani, the Iraqi government did not keep the peace agreement nor give the Kurds their autonomy.

In early spring of 1974, the Kurds and the Iraqi Armed Forces began to clash; as such, the Iraqi government imprisoned and executed thousands of Kurds opposing the regime. This time, my father and my uncle fled to the Iranian border and settled in the town of Choman with the *Peshmerga* to fight against the Iraqi regime. They fled for a few months before we all reunited. My mother only found out after she received a hand-delivered letter about his whereabouts, and in the letter, he asked her to leave Erbil with the children and join him on the border. Once again, we—along with hundreds of other Kurdish families—fled our homes, fearing for our lives because of the Iraqi regime.

One day when we returned from school, my mother told us that we were going to leave Erbil for a short time and that we need to pack very light. I remember the name of the town we were going to travel to, Shaqlawa, Erbil Governorate, fifty kilometers northeast of Erbil, between Safeen and Sorik Mountains. Kurds are the majority in Shaqlawa, though there is an Assyrian minority living there as well. Shaqlawa is considered a resort town because it is cool in the summer, drawing thousands of tourists from other parts of Iraq.

This was the place that we were supposed to travel to with no other explanation from my mother. The only thing we knew was that my mother, siblings, cousin, and another Kurdish woman whose family had fled earlier was going on this journey with us. The next day, we packed very light, got into taxis, and drove to Shaqlawa. We were greeted by family friends who were Christian. They were very hospitable as I remember, and they had cooked for us since they were expecting us. We rested until dark.

After we ate dinner and rested, my mother told us that we needed to make another trip, but this time, we were going to walk. "Walk where?" I said out loud. I was told that it was going to be a short trip to meet up with my father. A man was at this house when we got there; he was a *Peshmerga*, and he was sent by my father to help us escape. I remember being told to wear clothes that won't attract attention and that we had to be very careful when we walked, not to make any noise. I recall that evening we kept walking and walking until sunrise. At sunrise we rested. We were only kids—what did we know? We were asking my mother, "Are we there yet?" I remember the woman that came with us from Erbil was yelling at us, telling us to be quiet and that we were almost there.

I remember seeing helicopters flying over the area, and the *Peshmerga* guide telling us that these are Iraqi helicopters looking for people. He then told us we had to stay put and not move when these helicopters were flying overhead so that they don't spot us; otherwise they were going to bomb us. Well, from that moment, we were at once inaudible when we saw them flying. The *Peshmerga* guiding us to Choman where my father was was very nice and compassionate. This *Peshmerga* told us the Iraqi regime laid land mines in order to kill people escaping on foot. Needless to say, we were even more scared. Was there anything else we needed to know!

My mother is one of the strongest and bravest women I have ever known. My mother married my father at the age of thirteen as it was then custom to arrange a girl's marriage at a very young age. My parents had four girls and two boys who are all married with children now. My mother is still alive and lives in Tennessee, but my father died of a heart attack at age 65 in 1995.

Me with my father 1989 In Nashville.

We should have been playing and getting spoiled with toys instead of being entertained by the fact that helicopters were flying over us and carefully walking to avoid land mines! No one should ever go through what we have been through. I was only in my teens when I had to go through this ordeal. I was a teenager and I had fled my home twice, leaving behind all of our belongings. No one knew that this trip would turn into a week-long journey on foot nightly due to constant bombardment during the day. We traveled at night only, hiding under trees and rocks during the day to avoid Iraqi aircraft. No one knew exactly where the mines were, as they were not marked. The *Peshmerga* guide understood that the Iraqi aircraft were flying overhead and looking for refugees fleeing toward the border. As such, he was very good at avoiding aircraft detection but continued to warn us to be watchful of land mines and listened for aircraft during this journey.

After seven restless days and six nights, we got to an area that was controlled by the *Peshmerga*. We saw a few men approach us. At first, we were alarmed as they were armed gunman; in addition, they did not know who we were, so we were all very concerned. The *Peshmerga* guide who was traveling with us told them who we were (as my father was well-known among his group); after that, they told us to rest. The only place to rest was under a tree, with rocks as pillows! These *Peshmerga* called it home.

The *Peshmerga* were very gracious and sympathetic to us since we were mostly children, aside from my mother and the other lady. They brought us dry bread and a big bowl of soup. As I recall, it was not very good, but it was all they had and I was extremely hungry. During our journey, we did not always have the opportunity to eat. While walking along the road, we only got to eat what the nearby villages would sell to us; however, sometimes they did not have enough food for everyone. We either went without or made the portions smaller. After resting a few hours, my father appeared. We ran to him, hugged him, and hung onto him as love-starved children who needed his presence, protection, and guidance. It felt wonderful to see him.

My father was elated we arrived safely and unharmed. He did not want to be separated from us again, and it was very comforting to us to hear him say that. The next day, we all went to Choman, on the Iraqi-Iranian border. At the time, Choman was one of the main places where cross-border trade took place between the two countries. My father was close to my now husband, and they found us a house next to a stream that made my mother very happy. My husband was a Kurdish broadcaster for the Voice of Kurdistan at that time. He had fled earlier for the same reason as we all did. I found it very reassuring to see *Peshmerga* all around us. They were well armed, which made us feel safe. While we were in Choman, tensions began to escalate between the United States and Iraq.

The United States and Shah Reza Pahlavi of Iran, pro-Western, encouraged the Kurdish leadership to rise against the Iraqi regime, and in return, Iran would provide Kurds with logistical support, funds, and weapons. Mustafa Barzani took advantage of this opportunity, not knowing Iran's full motivations. It is worth noting, one of the factors contributing to the opposition between Iran and Iraq was the control of the Shatt al-Arab, an important channel for oil exports of both countries. It is the narrow waterway that forms the southern border between Iran and Iraq.

In 1975 during the OPEC conference, Saddam and the Shah of Iran agreed to settle their differences and signed a treaty, known as the Algiers Agreement. In this treaty, Iraq formally acceded to Iranian territorial demands, and in return, the Shah would cut off all aid to Kurdish revolutionaries. Along with US President Gerald Ford, Secretary of State Henry Kissinger approved this agreement that marked the end of Kurdish autonomy in Iraq. Kissinger helped create one of the darkest and the bloodiest era, the most painful period in the history of Kurdistan's struggle for obtaining basic human rights and freedom. In cooperation with Iran and Israel, Kissinger's plan for the Kurds, according to Koohzad, "was a ruthless, deceitful process, which resulted in hundreds of thousands of Kurds being slaughtered and displaced over the years." After signing the

Algiers Agreement, the Iraqi government started more waves "of Arabization by moving Arabs to the oil fields of Kurdistan, particularly those around Kirkuk."

Between 1975 and 1978, the Iraqi government deported thousands of Kurds who stayed behind into southern Iraq. A few of the single Kurdish educated men fled to Western European countries and were subsequently granted political asylum. They worked vigorously to create Kurdish lobbies in Europe that established contacts with Western politicians and the media. These lobbies also attempted to communicate their message internationally about the Kurdish situation and their suffering.

These political maneuvers left Mullah Mustafa powerless; as a result, he pled with the United States for help, but the United States did nothing to help the Kurds due to the agreement they had with Iraq and Iran. The Iraqi government started to demolish Kurdish villages and threaten thousands of Kurds. Hundreds of thousands of Kurds were deported and scattered to other parts of Iraq, helpless. I still remember those days because, at that time, we were living in the camps on the Iraq-Iran border as it was yesterday. After the Kurdish revolution collapsed, Mustafa Barzani came to Washington, DC, for medical reasons. Sadly, on March 1, 1979, he lost his battle with cancer. His sons, Idris Mustafa who died in 1987 of a heart attack and Masoud Barzani, the current president of Kurdistan Regional Government (KRG), led and continues to lead the party.

In 1975, Iranian officials set up camps in various areas on their border for Kurdish families who fled Iraq, but did not allow us to enter Iran. My family relocated to a camp near Urmia. During the Shah Pahlavi dynasty (1925–1979), the city was called Rezaiyeh. The population is predominantly Azerbaijani and Kurdish with Assyrian and Armenian minorities. Urmia was and still is a trade center because it is located in a fertile agricultural region where fruits such as grapes, apples, and tobacco are grown. In Urmia, we lived in tents the whole year. It was there where we learned that my great-grandfather was actually from that area! We reunited with our relatives whom we had never met or heard of before.

Both Iraq and Iran have hot summers and very cold winters, so this move was very harsh. For my mother, this move meant we washed and drank from the river nearby. It was not ideal, but we made the best of the situation. The Iranian government provided us with food and other essentials; in addition, they set up temporary schools in a run-down building (some sort of barrack). We started to learn a new language, Farsi.

Shortly thereafter, the Iraqi regime announced that they were issuing amnesty for the Kurds who fled to Iran or other border countries. Because of the amnesty announcement, my uncle decided to take his family back to Iraq because he did not like the life in the camps. Who would blame him? My father, on the other hand, refused to go back to Iraq and live under Saddam's regime. He begged his brother to stay, but he did not listen and returned to Iraq. My uncle packed his belongings along with his family, got into an Iraqi army truck that was sent by the Iraqi government, and went back to Iraq. Like my uncle, thousands of other Iraqi Kurds returned to Iraq in this same way. This was the last time I saw or heard of him ever again.

Even though I was just a teenager when all this was happening, I can still remember the constant sorrow and fear on everyone's faces. Fortunately, my parents were smart enough not to believe the Iraqi government's empty promises, so they stayed behind in a refugee camp with thousands of other Kurds.

In the meantime, and mostly due to the pressure from the international community, the Iranian government allowed the Iraqi Kurds that were still in camps to move into cities. They provided buses to move the Kurds into the various cities. Once settled, they provided refugees with homes and other living essentials.

In mid-1975, my family settled in Karaj, a city that is situated about twenty kilometers west of Tehran at the foothills of the Elborz Mountains. The majority of the population in the city are ethnic Persians; there are also Persianized Azerbaijanis, Lurs, and Kurds. Karaj is the fifth largest city in Iran. Many immigrants migrated there. Karaj is considered a tourist destination, famous for the beautiful Elborz Mountains.

Once again, we had to make new friends with the locals. By now, we had learned enough Farsi to take care of our immediate needs. However, we were still refugees, but now living in Karaj, instead of in tents and camps. It seemed like we were once again living in civilization! Although we were homesick and missed our friends and families, there seemed to be no choice. We had to try to live as normally as we could. My parents enrolled us in school. The Iranian people are very warm, gracious, and friendly; but when it came to religion, they were very strict and did not accept Sunni Muslims, often a point of contention.

The Shi'a totally dominates Iranian society, not only as a faith but also politically. About 90 percent of all Iranians are Shi'a, and the remaining are Sunni Muslims, Baha'i, and Christian. Additionally, there are also small communities likes Jews and even others who follow different religions that are much older than Islam. Because of their rigid beliefs, I did not tell my classmates that I was Sunni. Sometimes when asked about religion, I would lie and say that I was Shi'a so that I would be accepted and left alone. As time went by, my schoolmates found out that we were Sunni, but our friendships did not change because we had made positive impressions. In fact, two of my classmates continued to write even after I immigrated to the United States. Unfortunately, the letters stopped coming when the Shah of Iran was removed from power and the Khomeini/Islamic revolution took hold.

While living in Iran, my mother gave birth to a baby girl. In Iran, my father was reunited with an old family friend who would several years later ask for my hand in marriage. In the past, parents would arrange marriages when their children were born and they had to abide by this arrangement when the children grew up. This is less and less common today.

Pê-guhurk, which means exchange, is also a common practice in Kurdish marriages. This entails a direct exchange of girls—a sister/daughter of one man for the sister/daughter of another man. For example, if a wife had died, her widowed husband would exchange his daughter or sister for another wife instead of giving a dowry.

All my cousins were back in Iraq, so the pressure of marrying a cousin for us was never a consideration. We were safe from that fate. However, both my parents were very nationalistic and would not have accepted us girls marrying anyone other than a Kurd. It is much easier for men than women to marry a non-Kurd. The reason behind that is when a girl marries someone other than a Kurd, their children take up their father's names, and the woman loses part of her identity.

In May of 1976, a couple of my soon-to-be relatives came to our house and brought a clergyman (Imam) with them to marry us in an Islamic ceremony—similar to Westerners' engagement, without intimacy until you actually move from your parents' house to your husband's house. A wedding date was set for the following August but without wedding invitations or a celebration. Facing the new reality of my situation, I went along with my parents' decision. In my situation, if I chose not marry him, nothing would have happened to me because my parents were not ones to commit honor crimes or other draconian acts to their daughters who went against family orders, unfortunately common in some traditional families. That said, some Middle Eastern families still believe in forced marriages, or there could be ramifications to such a rejection, such as beatings, honor crimes, or stoning. I am fortunate my parents were never like that.

Having no control over my destiny is one thing, but how could I expect to spend the rest of my life with a man I knew nothing about? Naturally, I was terrified! I did not know what was expected of me. I had never held a real conversation with this man who was soon to be my husband. Traditionally the groom and his family provides a dowry, which is cash that accompanies the bride to her new home and serves as her financial security. This is a type of ancient prenuptial agreement. In today's urban Kurdistan, weddings are full of joy, fabulous parties, elegant Kurdish clothes, and of course, heirloom jewels that the groom buys for his wife. My situation, however, was different. We were refugees living in Iran. The majority of our families were back in Kurdistan. Both my parents decided on the spot that he was a good match. They liked him a lot, and they were old friends.

They knew my husband from Aqrah, where he was living with my family and going to school since his village did not have any schools.

There was something about his character my parents found charming. Never mind what I thought. I married a man of my parents' choice. I had met him once while we were in Erbil and a couple of times in Choman, where he was a broadcaster working for the Kurdish radio station Voice of Kurdistan.

Actually, I never even imagined getting married, but I guess you cannot run away from what fate has in store for you. I was raised to think a suitable man was one who was approved by my parents. While Western teenagers spent summers working and taking vacations with their friends, I spent my time learning to cook and hoping that someday, I would become a successful wife, mother, and independent woman.

In August 1976, my husband came to pick me up and take me to go to his home in Yazd to live happily ever after. I was anxious about moving to another city with a man who still seemed like a stranger. I was giving up my childhood and my family to be with a man I had only met a few times.

Let me summarize my early dating experiences. The first time I met my future husband was in the mid-'70s, when he visited my parents in Erbil. The second time I saw him was in Choman when we fled; the third time I saw him was in camp on the Iraq-Iran border, and the fourth time I saw him was in Karaj, when we became engaged. By the fifth occasion, we were married, without ever even having a full-length conversation once!

My husband was born in 1948, in the Zebar region of Aqrah. In 1970, he graduated from Mosul University with a BA in economics and worked briefly in Erbil. However, soon after that, he joined the *Peshmerga* and began his career as a news broadcaster at the Voice of Kurdistan.

He was definitely a Kurdish nationalist and was one of the Kurdish refugees who fled the Iraqi regime just like us. He left all his family behind except one married sister and a few cousins who were also refugees living in Iran. But he was Zebari! A Zebari! However, he was not from that same part of the Zebari family that had destroyed our lives. He came from a good family and was a decent man. He was and still is a loving and nurturing husband and father.

In August 1976, we got married, but we did not have the formal celebration that normally takes place afterward because we were refugees and both our extended families were in Iraq. We went for a short honeymoon in Tehran, the capital of Iran, and then went to Esfahan

What can I say about Esfahan? It was the most beautiful city I had ever seen. After two weeks in Esfahan, we still did not see all the sights of this marvelous city. "Esfahan is well-known for its architectural wonders and gardens. One of several familiar sights of Esfahan is the former royal mosque, now called Masjid-ê-Imam, from the 17th century, one of the best examples of Persian architecture." During the time we were in Esfahan, we went to the mosque a couple of times with two of my husband's close friends. After two weeks in this amazing city and the sightseeing, it was time to head home to Yazd where my husband lived and worked as a teacher. While driving to Yazd, seeing the nineteenth-century bazaar was incredibly exciting. Yazd was full of sights that are worth seeing, such as the ongoing fire temple that has been burning continually for thousands of years.

After a short while, I became aware of my husband's likes and dislikes. I discovered that he was a firm advocate for social equality between men and women. It was a relief to know that my life was not going to be bad, especially when I told him that I wanted to continue with my education. He strongly supported the idea. Education has always been important in Kurdish families, highly valued and respected within the community. Parents strongly encourage and support their children to get an education as much as possible.

Although I missed my family, after a few weeks, I got used to living in Yazd. Soon after, I found out that I was pregnant. I was petrified, and this was made even worse because I had no idea what to expect and had no family around me. Thankfully, my husband thought it was best that I go back and visit my mother in Karaj until I gave birth. I took his advice and went back to Karaj. On July 11, 1977, just after turning sixteen, I gave birth to a beautiful, healthy baby girl, and my husband chose to give her a Kurdish name. Tell the joke about how your daughter is still upset she was born in Iran!

After one week of giving birth, my husband came to Karaj. At the same time, he suddenly informed me that we were to move to the United States. My husband told me that he cannot live in Iran because it was as bad as Iraq for Kurds. I knew that we were restricted in Iran because for the most part, we required permission to go from one city to another; Iraqi Kurds were treated like outlaws.

On the way back to Yazd, my husband tried to convince me why we should move to the United States. In truth, his reasons were legitimate and obvious. He could no longer tolerate how Kurds were treated. I was saddened to hear that he made up his mind and that I would be leaving behind my family. I did not want to be separated from my family even though we lived in two different cities. However, I was still able to visit because we were still in one country. My husband's application to the United States had been approved and we were leaving very soon.

Being a new mother and all these changes were very difficult for me. Girls my age in America enjoyed many freedoms, while I opted for motherhood and worked on learning how to become a good wife, not an easy task since I was still trying to get to know my husband!

When we arrived back in Yazd from Karaj, we started packing, and two weeks later, we headed back to Karaj and stayed with my family one last time. Two days later, we went to the airport in Tehran. My parents came along with us to say good-bye. Once again, I was separated from my family. I sensed it was going to be for a very long time before I saw them again. I was right. I did not see my family again until eleven years later, in 1984. I was very emotional at that time, but I had to do what fate had planned for me.

We had been offered political asylum in the United States, along with many other Kurds who wanted to get out of Iran and be free.

After a few long hours, we landed in Frankfurt, Germany. We were told that we had to stay at the hotel that they had provided for all of us until all the immigration paperwork was completed. Here we were with a few other Iraqi Kurdish families trying to find a better life far away from the oppressive Iraqi and the Iranian regimes.

With my husband, daughter, and son in Memphis, TN, 1984.

While we were in Germany, the United States issued us green cards. When we received these, we were told that we will be going to the United States the next day. We headed to New York and, many hours later, landed at JFK airport. I felt overwhelmed. I was especially afraid of my future. We stayed in New York City for one night, and then each family had an assigned sponsor.

Our sponsor was Catholic Charities. They were located in Nashville, Tennessee, famously known as the home of the Grand Ole Opry and country music. The sponsors helped new arrivals to settle, find living accommodations, get children enrolled in school, and get families resettled and welcomed in their new location. We were very blessed to have their assistance because without their help, we would have been lost. I want to mention them because I am very appreciative of the help they provided during the time when we were in desperate need.

During 1976–1977, Catholic Charities sponsored many Kurdish refugees fleeing Iraq. They took us in and gave us choices where to live. My husband chose Nashville because two of his cousins had already come to Nashville a year earlier. He thought it would be better to have somebody rather than nobody. So we settled in Nashville, and boy, did we have a hard time understanding the country accents at first! We ended up living there for sixteen years.

I had never met my husband's cousins living in Nashville. They had already enrolled in school, were making good progress, become adapted to the culture, and learned English well. The day we arrived in Nashville, my daughter turned forty days old. I was very nervous and anxious to be alone, far away from my family, and a new mother. After a few weeks of experiencing the culture shock, I decided to talk to our sponsor through a translator about enrolling in an English as a second language (ESL) class, and so I did.

After just a few months, I was able to communicate with my neighbors, but only in a limited way. My husband already had a college degree from Iraq, but I still had to finish high school. English was not a strange language to me because we had to take it in school while in Iraq. However, living in the south was often a challenge. I felt it was a different language than English. Even so, I managed to learn and understand it after just a few months. I was excited and eager to learn and be able to speak it fluently.

To make friends, I went to school and visited libraries. Soon I discovered that having an arranged marriage was not so bad, and in fact, telling my story was an icebreaker when meeting new friends. Although it was difficult for the American girls my age to understand that arranged marriage was not so bad, it was not as difficult as I imagined. I liked the fact that I had married a Kurdish man who understood my upbringing and culture.

The next step I felt was necessary was to get a driver's license so that I did not have to depend on my husband. On my first attempt, I was able to pass the exam and received my license! I was particularly happy because I felt self-sufficient. Meanwhile, my husband was enrolled in school hoping to get his master's degree; but after only one year, he decided to quit and work full-time to support the family.

I continued to go to school and received an associate of science degree in computer programming and worked in the computer field for one year. I was not happy doing the same job every day. I was bored. I left that job and decided to try another profession. I registered for nursing at one of the local universities. I attended classes during the day and worked as a pharmacy technician at a local hospital at night. After I graduated, I started to work with a pediatric group for two years as a nurse. Within the nursing field, I changed my specialty to internal medicine and worked with an internist for three years. I later switched to work in dermatology.

In the meantime, my family was still living in Iran. I had submitted an application to the Immigration and Naturalization Service (INS), now called United States Citizenship and Immigration Services (USCIS), to have my family come to the United States. One day in 1983, I received a call from Catholic Charities, and they informed me that my family left Iran and have temporarily been settled in Rome, Italy. They gave me a number to call them. I called, and my father answered. I was so happy to hear his voice! I had not heard his voice in a very long time. I then spoke with my mother, sisters, and brother. I frequently called and talked to them over the next six months.

After that half of a year, I received another call from my father saying that their paperwork had arrived and that they have been accepted to come to the United States. I was extremely happy! I had not seen them for almost twelve years. In 1984, on the day that they were to arrive in Nashville, I went to the airport to pick up my family. I thought it was a dream. I could not believe that this was true.

I arrived at the airport two hours early and waited anxiously for their plane to land. Once I looked up, I saw my father—wow, what a feeling! I then saw my mother, followed by my sisters and brother. We were hugging and crying. It was a very emotional moment for me.

When I last saw them, I was only sixteen years old—but by the time they arrived, I had two children since I gave birth to a boy in 1980. I brought my family home with me, and they stayed with me until I was able to find them a place of their own. After a couple of weeks, I was able to find them a house nearby, and I visited them every day. Life was good again, with the exception of one brother who had gone to Denmark to settle. Even so, I had my parents, three sisters, and one brother, and nothing or no one was going to separate us again.

In 1988, Saddam Hussein started another campaign against the Kurds and called it *Anfal*, meaning "the spoils." This name is also the eighth Sura (chapter) in the Qur'an. The Iraqi military took heavy actions against the Iraqi Kurds by gassing them with chemicals, which started in February and ended in September 1988. According to many censuses sources, there were five thousand innocent Kurdish men, women, and children killed and many more injured and badly affected by the chemical exposure during one particularly brutal day. In addition, hundreds of thousands of Kurdish civilians were forcibly removed from their homes, and their villages were destroyed. This well-known incident occurred in the Kurdish town of Halabja. Some people have been physically deformed, and some have also lost their mental abilities due to these chemical agents. Kurds carry the mental scar of this tragedy. It will never be forgotten.

On the evening of March 21, 1988, we were celebrating Newroz, the Kurdish New Year, in Nashville, when we received the news of this most tragic and ghastly crime against the Kurds once again. The Iraqi government had once again shown us clear and obvious evidence of their hatred toward Kurdish people. It was an organized attempt by the Iraqi regime under Saddam Hussein to eradicate Kurdish efforts toward political independence. I did not know that several years later, I would find myself interviewing the victims of this tragedy for my job.

On February 15, 1991, US President George Bush announced that the United States would fight the Iraqi government to protect Kuwait against Saddam Hussein. He asked the Kurds in the north and the Shi'a in the south to revolt against Saddam and promised US support in return. The Kurds were especially happy to learn that the United States was encouraging uprisings against the Iraqi regime. They were expecting full support in their efforts against the government. Little did they know that the help they were promised would not be fulfilled.

The Kurds were disappointed, but they should have learned their lesson from the Algiers Agreement when Kissinger let them down. A similar uprising took place in the south where the Iraqi government killed many Shi'a Arabs and destroyed their lands. Afterward, Saddam forcedly relocated those Arabs and drained their ancient marshlands.

My husband has a passion for poetry. He composed a powerful poem on this tragedy called "*Bo Kê Bikim Gazî û Hawar*" ("Who Shall I Call or Turn To") that was later turned into a beautiful, yet heartbreaking song by Mahabad Ibrahim, a famous female Kurdish singer. This was his cry when we heard of the tragic news of the gassing of the Kurds and saw unforgettable images on television of Kurds running for their lives, climbing barefoot in the mountains, throwing their babies off mountains because they could not care for them, leaving the elderly behind because they could not carry on the journey of walking to the nearest border of Turkey or Iran for safe haven. Here's a line from this poem: "Who should I call or turn to? Should I turn to the same cold, frozen conscience, or to the deaf and silent world?"

My husband's first collection of poems was published in 1999 called *Werê Şêran* (*The Land of Lions*). Although all his formal education was in Arabic, he taught himself to read and write Kurdish. While still in high school, he began writing poetry in Kurdish. His poetry is mostly about love, Kurdistan, Kurdish society, politics, and culture. While in high school, he wrote his first poem called "Nesrin." This poem that was later composed to music and sang by the well-known Kurdish singer Mohammed Sexo (Mohammed *Sêxo*). This song is one of the most beloved songs in all four parts of Kurdistan and is a favorite among Kurdish singers even today.

In 1992, my husband got a job with Voice of America, in Washington, DC. I encouraged him to take it since working in radio was his passion. I was working, had a nice home, and my family was in Tennessee, and it was easy for me to encourage him to take this job. I did not find it feasible for us to pack and move right away until he was settled in his new job.

My husband Khalaf Zebari, at The Voice of America 2010.

One year later, we decided that it was time to sell our home in Nashville and move to Washington, DC, once it was determined that the job was secure and government funding for the Kurdish station was going to continue. Once more, I left my parents behind. After a few weeks of settling in, we enrolled our children in middle and high school, and I got a job at one of the local hospitals.

On December 18, 1995, I had just come home from work when I received a call from my brother in Nashville saying that our father had passed away from a heart attack. I was devastated and immediately booked a flight and flew to Nashville. When I got there, I was traumatized. I loved my father very much, and I was sad to see him go after we had been reunited.

Before my father's death earlier that year, my father had been actively petitioning Muslims in the Nashville area to donate money to the local mosque to purchase a piece of land for a burial ground since at that time there was none for Muslims. He had kept a diary of who contributed and who did not. I was told that a few days earlier, he had gone to the mosque to hand over the money that he had collected, and the Imam of the mosque had asked him what the rush was. My father apparently had said, "I have a feeling that I am going to be the first one to be buried at this cemetery."

Indeed, my father was the first one to be buried there. The land was still not approved by the zoning commission when my father had passed. It took a few calls to get this permit, and after ten days, my father was laid to rest at this cemetery. According to Islam, the deceased must be buried as soon as possible after death. However, it was not possible since the land had not been approved, and my brother from Denmark had not yet arrived. We were not willing to disregard my father's wish to be buried in a Muslim cemetery.

The death of a loved one is an extremely painful and emotional time. Generally speaking, the loved ones of a deceased person observe a forty day mourning period in Islam. During the forty days, visitors come and bring food and family and friends pay visits to the grave site. I stayed with my mother for one month, and while there, I had several episodes of anxiety attacks. When I returned home to Washington, DC, I decided not to resume my profession as a nurse. It was a reminder of my father's death, and I could no longer handle seeing another sick patient or death. Later that year, I registered at a university and studied psychology, hoping to become a multicultural counselor. After I graduated, I worked in family services where I helped hundreds of refugee families who fled Bosnia and Herzegovina, people who similarly suffered trauma of war and displacement.

This office provided employment counseling and job placement to newly arrived refugees and immigrants in the area. I was a Family Service Worker, who works with clients on various kinds of employment-related issues, including job applications, job placement/referrals, and counseling on work adjustment. Whenever I interviewed the refugees, I remembered my own ordeal and how I started just like them.

In 1997, Voice of America needed a part-time broadcaster to deliver health-related programs promoting the vaccination of children in the rural areas where Kurds lived. Knowing that Kurds constantly listened to the news on shortwave radio (which in many cases was the only means they had to obtain news in Kurdish), I decided to give it a try until they found a suitable applicant. I enjoyed it very much and ended up working there on weekends while I still maintained my regular job with Family Services until 2000.

In 2000, my husband, daughter, and I decided to go back to Kurdistan to visit our family. I had not seen my homeland since 1974 and did not know what would be waiting for us upon our return. We flew to Diyarbakir, Turkey, where we did not feel welcomed at all. The airport security was not friendly, and we were interrogated by Turkish officials, simply because we were Kurds. My daughter was very scared and wanted to go back to America. We had arranged for a car to drive us to Kurdistan. After a few hours, we arrived at the border, which was between Silopi and Zakho. I recall a story that I heard when I got to Silopi. I was told not to mention the word *Kurdistan* because the country does not exist. "Instead tell them that you're going to Iraq even though they know Zakho is a Kurdish city, otherwise, the border patrols will reject your visa for wrongful entry and make you go back where you came from."

This was also the first time I would meet my husband's immediate family (his brothers); I had only met one of his sisters and mother for a week prior to getting married. When we arrived at Zakho, they were waiting for us. I found them to be very warm and very friendly.

Seeing the orchards, the mountains, and the beautiful scenery brought back childhood memories as we were driving toward my birthplace of Aqrah, where my husband's family lived. When we arrived at Aqrah, we rested for a bit, but I was anxious to go and see my family's old house. It was like déjà vu. We traveled throughout

Kurdistan, but of course, we could not go to the south since that region was still under the control of Saddam Hussein.

We stayed in Kurdistan for one month and traveled to as many towns and areas as we could. It was breathtaking! When we returned to Aqrah, I ate as many pomegranates and figs as I could—Aqrah is famous for those fruits. We saw our distant family and cousins, whom I barely remembered, but I was happy to have seen them again. At that time, I also took many photos and gathered as much information as I could about my family's past tragedy from my aunts and cousins. It was hard to say good-bye to my family and return to America.

In 2002, President George Bush named Iraq as part of an "axis of evil." I sensed something was about to happen. My instincts were right because I received an e-mail from a government contractor who offered me a job that was too hard to turn down. This position was at the Department of the State and entailed traveling to interview victims of the chemical bombardment on Halabja. For this cause, I took a leave of absence from my job in social services at the request of the Department of State. Thankfully, my employer approved and was happy to lend me for this opportunity knowing my background. I was eager to start showing the world Saddam's cruelty. The aim was to gather enough evidence to bring Saddam Hussein to the International Court for his ghastly actions toward the Kurdish people as well as others.

I still remember some of the people we interviewed. They hold us about that appalling day they had witnessed. Some of those people were disfigured; some were not able to carry a child to full term due to the effect the chemicals they had been exposed to. As they were telling me their story, I felt that I was with them; I was feeling the same feelings, hearing the same sounds that they had experienced. I recall every one of those people telling me that at first they smelled an odor like sour apples—which, they explained, seemed pleasant at first. As we were conducting these interviews and taking down their stories, we were told that after just a few seconds of this odor, people and animals started to fall, and birds began to fall from the sky. Even flowers started to wilt in an unnatural way.

After a few days in Europe, we gathered enough documents and conducted enough interviews for a long report. After several months of traveling abroad, this project successfully came to an end. I returned back to my position in social services and was immediately promoted. However, after a few months, the same government contractor called me about another opportunity. This time, it was to head the recruiting department to recruit linguists for many different Middle Eastern languages.

My job was very demanding and required working long hours. In the meanwhile, my daughter was engaged to be married, and I was required to help. Between my demanding job, long hours, and the ever-ringing cell phone, I still somehow managed to help her plan her wedding. In January 2003, she got married, and the wedding was fabulous!

In the spring of 2003, then president George W. Bush decided to take action against Saddam Hussein once and for all. The Americans needed Turkish assistance to let US troops pass through Turkey into Iraq; however, the Turkish Parliament rejected the request, so the United States asked the Iraqi Kurdish leaders for their assistance in this matter. The Kurdish leaders welcomed the United States's request with open arms, and the Kurdish *Peshmerga* forces helped alongside the US forces to remove the Iraqi tyrant, so the United States received more than they had bargained for. The American forces that were deployed to Iraqi Kurdistan enjoyed Kurdish hospitality and serenity, while those in the south were harassed, kidnapped, and killed.

In April 2003, I was required to go to Iraq and help the site manager recruit local national linguists to help our troops abroad. Groups of people were required to travel with me to help. We had to go for safety training in another state, and it lasted ten days. After that long ten days, we flew to Kuwait and stayed there for a month until we received word that it was safe for us to go to Iraq.

Me in Mosul 2003.

In May 2003, I had been given a satellite telephone and an SUV to drive to Iraq from Kuwait with a convoy for protection. When we got to the Iraqi border, I saw Iraqi Bedouins on the road waiting for the US troops to give them food and water. I was angry because God allowed Saddam Hussein to be so evil and make his own people suffer. They were hungry and were approaching us for food and water. While driving along this desert, I was ambushed several times; but the last time I was ambushed, I really thought that was the end for me.

In December 2003, one of my colleagues, a former Special Forces soldier and I had to drive to Erbil to check one of our many sites. I had traveled to Baghdad, Najaf, Karbala, Samara, Tikrit, and many other towns in the south. While driving back to Mosul from Erbil, we were at a traffic circle when a four-door Toyota sedan pulled in front us and blocked our vehicle. The driver exited the vehicle and approached the driver's side of our vehicle. I assessed his actions as hostile and responded. My colleague, who was driving, reversed the car a few feet and jumped the curb into the center of the traffic circle. Once he was over the curb, he went forward and got around the vehicle. The other driver then produced a pistol and fired three shots into the rear of our vehicle. Two shots struck the rear's lower part of the passenger side, one through the license plate and the other in the quarter panel. We made a high-speed escape at that time. We managed to get ahead of the shooter by about two hundred yards.

We had to slow for traffic, and at that time, he caught back up with us. When he got close, my colleague slammed on to the brakes to throw him off. He locked up his brakes and slid sideways. Traffic was at a standstill, so he jumped the curb and headed into oncoming traffic. Once we got far enough ahead of him, we switched back to the correct lane of traffic. As we were trying to find our way back to the friendly lanes, we were crossing an overpass when an improvised explosive device (IED) exploded. Miraculously, we did not receive any damage from the explosion. The IED was a total coincidence. If not for the shooter, we would not have traveled down the road where the IED exploded.

The incidents were reported to local military unit (MI). I was scared and felt like a bullet magnet. Every time I went out, something like this happened. After coming back to the office, we went back to check the bullet impacts. We traced the one bullet path through the license plate. It went through the back door, then through the rear seat, and ended up lodged in the satellite phone vehicle adapter. Of course, the adapter was destroyed.

Sadly, while I was in Iraq, I lost many coworkers and employees. A few of them were Kurdish. I had to greet families of the deceased who were returning from the United States to bury their loved ones in Kurdistan, where they wanted to be buried. While still completing my work in Iraq, I received a call from my company about another assignment in Norway at the US Embassy. I did not want to go back just then because I felt like my job was not yet completed in Iraq, but they insisted I return to the United States. I came back to the United States and rested for about a week.

In December 2004, I took a flight to Iceland, and from there, I hopped on another plane to Norway. Once I got there, I was greeted at the airport and was taken to a hotel. I started working the next day and ended up staying there for four months. While I was in Norway, I was fortunate enough to meet and work with many US officials who held high-ranking positions. I was asked if I could travel to Baghdad with them to help with some work that needed my expertise. I accepted to help them with the mission and met the team I was going to travel to Baghdad with, and we spent about ten days there.

We landed in Balad, which is about fifty miles north of Baghdad. We rested a bit and then hopped into a helicopter. I remember getting shot at from below at that time. I was petrified even though we had Norwegian security with us, but thankfully, nothing happened, and we arrived in Baghdad safely. When we arrived in Baghdad, we were taken to Baghdad central prison, the infamous Abu Ghraib, northwest of Baghdad International Airport. Saddam Hussein tortured and executed thousands of innocent people in this prison.

In 2003, after the fall of the former regime, the American forces in Iraq used Abu Ghraib as a detention center. I spent a total of ten days working in this prison. The prison, as well as other buildings nearby, were getting hit by RPGs (rocket-propelled grenades) almost every day I was there, and it was by the grace of God that I lived to tell my story. After ten long days, we returned to Norway, and I resumed my work at the embassy. Just before I was about to complete my mission in Norway, the director at the office I worked for told me that he was very impressed with the work I had performed and that he sent off my résumé to other US agencies and said the Department of Defense (DoD) would be in contact with me upon my return to the United States. I took it with a grain of salt since I was not looking for a new job; I was happy with the company I was working for.

After a long cold winter spent in Norway, I was happy to come home to the United States and return to my family. After a few days of rest, I reported back to work and was immediately promoted to an operations manager. After one week of my return, I received a call from a federal agency recruiter asking me to meet with her to discuss a job opportunity. She told me that I was referred to her by a colleague in Norway. I met with her the next day, and she told me about the position. At the time, I was not willing to travel anymore for work. I needed to be home with my family. I turned down the job. She told me that she forwarded my résumé to another local federal government agency and that I should expect a call from them. Indeed I did receive a call shortly after, and the position they had offered me was very exciting. I accepted the offer and had to pass all of their exams, which I did. I was very happy with the type of work I did.

After nine years working there, I had to take family leave because my husband was hospitalized for almost four months and spent most of his time in the intensive care unit (ICU). He was a heavy smoker and he developed chronic obstruction pulmonary disease (COPD) and had to be put on a ventilator due to the failure of his vital organs.

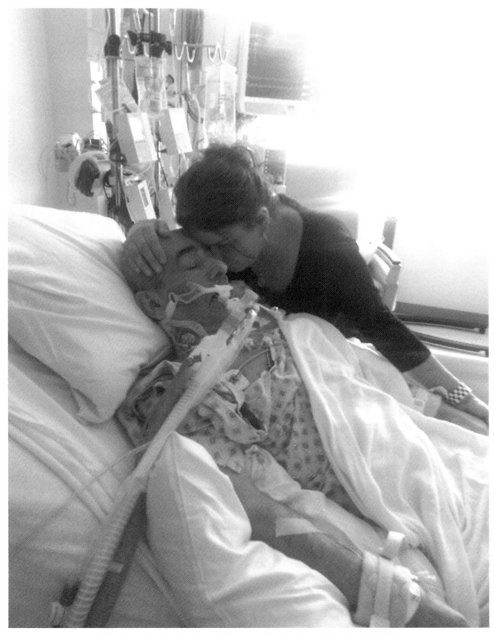

Me with my husband while on life support in 2013 at Fairfax Hospital ICU.

Thank God, he came out of it and recovered, but his memory is still suffering. As they say "you never know what God has in store." I had many plans, but at the end of the day, whatever God has in store for me was going to happen no matter what. I took time off from work and decided to take my husband back to Kurdistan to see his family since he recovered. In 2014, we took off and stayed for a couple of months. He was so happy to see his family although his memory had suffered due to his illness. He could not remember everyone's names or recognize faces. We traveled as much as he could handle and visited all his childhood places. One of which was Baniya the village in which he grew up. Below is a picture of this breathtaking place. It was indeed like heaven as he used to describe it to me.

Me looking over my birth city, Aqrah.

Me overlooking the nature and wishing that my father was alive to see it one more time.

For all that I endured, I am thankful to be an American and to be living here. There are so many reasons why I love the United States, my adopted country. I am so proud to say that. The first reason is personal freedom. The second reason includes several other freedoms, such as the freedom to worship, freedom of speech, freedom to pursue one's own happiness, and the freedom to live life on one's own terms.

The thing that I love the *most* about the United States is the American people and its diversity. I like the way in which people come to America, including people from all over the world who come here seeking freedom and a better life. The same people now believe in the American dream and continue to make this country great. God bless them all, and God bless America. I live in a proud country that stands tall in the face of threats, a country that fights fearlessly and stands for justice and freedom, which are not always taken without a price. I am proud to be an American and proud to be a Kurd.

Chapter 4

Kurdish Food

Kurdish cuisine is similar to other Middle Eastern cuisines, namely Persian, but also has maintains its own distinct dishes and spices. Kurdish meals use a variety of herbs and vegetables. Chicken and lamb are the primary meats, but we also occasionally eat seafood as well as beef. With combinations of herbs, spices, fresh fruits, and vegetables, I am certain that you and your loved ones will enjoy eating Kurdish food as much as my family does.

A Kurdish breakfast typically consists of flatbread called *naan*, yogurt, cheese, *tahin* (made from sesame seeds, similar to peanut butter), eggs, and of course, tea. You will find the same breakfast menu on Kurdish tables (called *sofrah* in Kurdish) everywhere regardless of where you are in Kurdistan. In Kurdistan, there are bakeries everywhere, and the bakeries specialize in certain kinds of bread, such as *lavash*, *dorik*, and *samoon*. Each morning, these bakeries provide freshly baked bread for the customers who frequent them daily.

For lunch, Kurds eat heavier meals than during dinnertime. They normally will prepare a full meal for lunch since the workday is shorter and many will return home to eat. For dinner, it will usually be something light or whatever is left over from lunch.

The following collection of recipes is a combination of traditional and altered dishes based on my own preferences. I always experiment with different spices and new ways of cooking or baking dishes. Earlier in my life, cooking to me was actually a burden because I did not know how to cook. Now that I have learned, I enjoy cooking and consider it even therapeutic at times and cathartic. I also love entertaining, especially on the weekends when everyone is home together. I hope you find this book educational and you discover some new favorite recipes!

ENTRÉES

White Rice (Pilaf/Palaw)

Rinse the rice with cold water until the water appears clear. Fill a pot with boiled water and add the rice with a pinch of salt. The salt will keep the rice from breaking. Leave the rice soaking in this water and salt at room temperature for at least 1 hour prior to cooking.

When you're ready to cook your rice, pour out all of the water from the rice and put the rice on the stove. Add 10 cups of boiled water with salt (to your taste) and stir gently and cover. Allow to boil on medium heat until the rice is firm to the bite (al dente), about 7 minutes. Remove the rice from the heat and pour into a fine strainer in the sink.

In the same pot, melt one stick of butter and add the rice back into the pot. Make a few holes in the rice with an end of a wooden spoon. Cut up the remaining ½ stick of butter and place the chunks of butter into these holes. Cover the pot with a paper towel, cheese cloth, or a towel to absorb moisture. Allow to cook slowly over low heat for 30 minutes.

This process will allow the rice to form a hard crust in the bottom ("Tahdeeg"). Scoop half a cup of rice from the top and into a small bowl. Add the dissolved saffron to this half cup of rice. Set aside. Once the rice is ready, place a large round platter on top of your pot and flip the pot onto the platter. Take off the top crunchy part of the rice (tahdig) and place in a separate plate. Gently pour the saffron mixture over the rice (not the tahdig) and serve with your choice of stew or soup. My favorite is the crust . . . it is crunchy.

4 cups uncooked long-grain basmati rice

7 cups water

1 teaspoon saffron (dissolved in 4 tablespoons of hot water)

1½ stick butter

Salt to taste

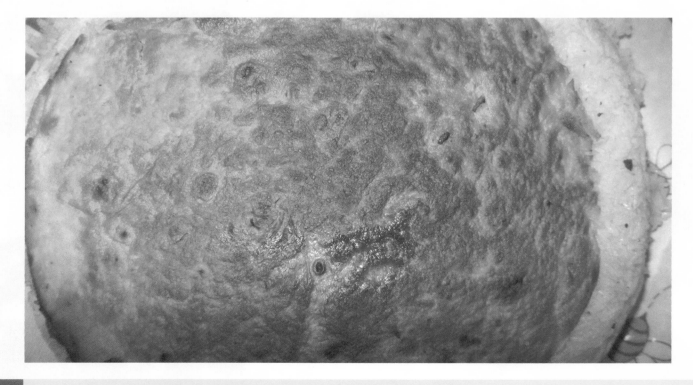

Carrot Rice

Rinse the rice with cold water until the water appears clear. Fill a pot with boiled water and add the rice with a pinch of salt. The salt will keep the rice from breaking. Leave the rice soaking in this water and salt at room temperature for at least 1 hour prior to cooking.

When you're ready to cook your rice, pour out all of the water from the rice and put the rice on the stove. Add 3 cups of boiled water with salt (to your taste) and stir gently and cover. Allow to boil on medium heat until the rice is firm to the bite (al dente), about 7 minutes. Remove the rice from the heat and pour into a fine strainer in the sink.

Heat ½ stick of butter in the same pot. Add the onions and sauté until golden brown. Add the shredded carrots, cinnamon, turmeric, and salt to taste; mix well. Add 1 cup chicken or beef broth and cook until the liquid has evaporated. Add the rice to this mix. Gently mix. Cover with a towel to simmer over low heat for 30 minutes. When rice is ready, pour the rice in a large platter. Serve with side dish of your choice.

1½ cups uncooked long-grain basmati rice
1 cup broth (chicken or beef)
2½ cups shredded carrots
1 cup chopped onion
1 teaspoon cinnamon
1 teaspoon turmeric
3 cups water
1 stick butter
Salt to taste

Cabbage Rice

Rinse the rice with cold water until the water appears clear. Fill a pot with boiled water and add the rice with a pinch of salt. The salt will keep the rice from breaking. Leave the rice soaking in this water and salt at room temperature for at least 1 hour prior to cooking.

When you're ready to cook your rice, pour out all of the water from the rice and put the rice on the stove. Add 6 cups of boiled water with salt (to your taste) and stir gently and cover. Allow to boil on medium heat until the rice is firm to the bite (al dente), about 7 minutes. Remove the rice from the heat and pour into a fine strainer in the sink.

In a skillet, brown the meat. Add onion and sauté until translucent. Add the spices and mix gently.

In a separate pan, sauté the cabbage in ½ stick of butter until wilted. Add the cabbage to the meat and mix well.

In the rice pot, melt ½ stick of butter. Add half of the cooked rice and gently flatten. Next add the cabbage and meat mixture, and then add the remaining rice. Cover the top of your pot with a paper towel or cheese cloth, place the lid on top, and simmer over low heat for 30 minutes. When rice is ready, pour the rice in a large platter. Serve with side dish such as *torshi, tzatziki,* or side salad.

3 cups uncooked long-grain basmati rice
½ pound ground beef
1 large onion, finely sliced
1 small head cabbage, shredded
1 stick butter
½ teaspoon turmeric
6 cups water
Salt and pepper to taste

Fava Bean Rice

Wash and rinse the rice. Wash and rinse the fava beans. Bring 5 cups of water to a boil with salt to taste. Add the rice and fava beans and mix gently. Allow to cook until the rice is firm to the bite (al dente), about 5–7 minutes. Drain the rice and beans.

In the same pot, melt ½ stick of butter and add rice/beans back. Add the dill. Mix gently. Make a few holes in the rice with an end of a wooden spoon. Cut up the remaining ½ stick of butter and place the chunks of butter into these holes. Cover the pot with a paper towel, cheese cloth, or a towel to absorb moisture. Allow to cook slowly over low heat for 30 minutes.

Serve with side dish such as torshi, tzatziki, or side salad.

2 cups uncooked long-grain basmati rice
1 small bag frozen fava beans
2 cups of dried dill
1 stick butter
5 cups water (keep one cup for later)
Salt and pepper to taste

Lentil Rice

Wash and rinse the rice. Bring 5 cups of water to a boil with salt to taste. Add the rice. Allow to cook until the rice is firm to the bite (al dente), about 5–7 minutes. Drain and set aside.

In same pot, wash and rinse the lentils. Bring 3 cups water to a boil and add the lentils with salt to taste. Allow to cook on medium heat for 15–20 minutes. Drain.

2 cups uncooked long-grain basmati rice
2 cups uncooked red lentils
1 pound ground beef
1 small onion, chopped
1 stick butter
5 cups water for rice, 3 cups for lentils
Salt and pepper to taste
1 cup yellow raisins (optional)

Melt ½ stick of butter in the same pot. Add the rice and layer with the lentils. Mix together gently. Cover the pot with a paper towel, cheese cloth, or a towel to absorb moisture. Allow to cook slowly over low heat for 30 minutes.

Serve with side dish such as torshi, tzatziki, or side salad.

Spinach Rice

Rinse the rice with cold water until the water appears clear. Fill a pot with boiled water and add the rice with a pinch of salt. The salt will keep the rice from breaking. Leave the rice soaking in this water and salt at room temperature for at least 1 hour prior to cooking.

When you're ready to cook your rice, pour out all of the water from the rice and put the rice on the stove. Add 6 cups of boiled water with salt (to your taste) and stir gently and cover. Allow to boil on medium heat until the rice is firm to the bite (al dente), about 7 minutes. Remove the rice from the heat and pour into a fine strainer in the sink.

Wash and rinse the chicken. Heat ½ cup of oil in same pot the rice was cooked in. Add the chicken and cook on both sides until golden brown. Remove the chicken from the pan and set aside.

Add the onions to the same pot and sauté until golden brown. Add the spinach, salt and pepper, and sauté until spinach is wilted. Mix gently. Add the chicken and mix gently. Pour the cooked rice on top of this mixture.

Heat the remaining oil in a small frying pan until sizzling hot. Pour this hot oil slowly over the rice. Do not mix. Cover the pot with a paper towel, cheese cloth or a towel to absorb moisture. Allow to cook slowly over low heat for 30 minutes.

Once the rice is ready, place a large round platter on top of your pot and flip the pot onto the platter.

Serve with side dish such as torshi, tzatziki, or side salad.

4 cups uncooked long-grain basmati rice
6 cups of water
2 bunches of fresh spinach (washed and chopped)
1 pound chicken breast (cut up) or skinless chicken thighs
1 medium-size onion, quartered
1 cup vegetable or canola oil
Salt and pepper to taste

Rice with Fish

Rinse the rice with cold water until the water appears clear. Fill a pot with boiled water and add the rice with a pinch of salt. The salt will keep the rice from breaking. Leave the rice soaking in this water and salt at room temperature for at least 1 hour prior to cooking.

When you're ready to cook your rice, pour out all of the water from the rice and put the rice on the stove. Add 6 cups of boiled water with salt (to your taste) and stir gently and cover. Allow to boil on medium heat until the rice is firm to the bite (al dente), about 7 minutes. Remove the rice from the heat and pour into a fine strainer in the sink.

Clean the fish. Season with salt, pepper, and turmeric. Heat oil in a nonstick pan and place the fish in the pan. Fry both sides for a few minutes until each side is golden. Pour the dissolved saffron and lemon juice over the fish. Cover and turn off the heat.

Melt the butter in the rice pot. Add the cooked rice and dried dill. Mix well. Cover on low heat for 20–30 minutes. Once the rice is ready, flip it over onto a large round platter. Remove the fish from the pan and add on top of the rice. This is good to serve with torshi or Kurdish salad.

6 fillets of white fish

3 cups uncooked long-grain basmati rice

3 cups dried dill

3 tablespoons vegetable or canola oil

1 stick of melted butter

½ teaspoon of saffron, dissolved in 1 tablespoon hot water

½ cup of lemon juice (or 1 large fresh-squeezed lemon)

1 teaspoon turmeric

6 cups water

Salt and pepper to taste

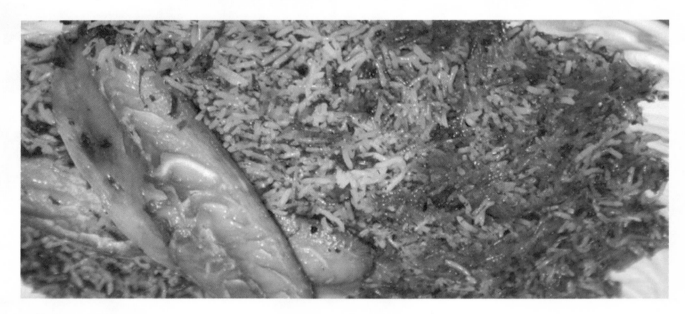

Kale Rice

Sauté onion and kale in a ¼ cup of oil until wilted.

Wash and rinse the rice. Place a pot on medium-high heat and bring broth (or water) to a boil. Add the rice and kale/onion mixture. Add turmeric, allspice, salt and pepper to your taste. Cover and cook on low heat for 10 minutes.

Heat remaining oil in a frying pan until sizzling hot. Pour this oil over the rice. Allow to cook on low for another 5–10 minutes.

Once the rice is ready, flip it over onto a large round platter. This is good to serve with tzatziki or Kurdish salad.

2 cups uncooked long-grain basmati rice
2 pounds kale, washed and chopped
1 large onion, chopped
3 cups chicken broth or water
1 tablespoon turmeric powder
1 teaspoon allspice
½ cup vegetable oil
Salt and pepper to taste

Chicken and Rice Casserole (Tah-Chin)

Wash and rinse rice. Transfer it to a nonstick pot and add five cups of water and salt to taste. Bring to a boil. Cook until al dente/firm to the bite, about 5–7 minutes. Drain the rice and leave in strainer.

In a frying pan, sauté onion in 1 tablespoon butter until golden brown. Add saffron and mix well. Add the yogurt, mix, and remove from heat.

In a separate small pan, sauté the barberries in two tablespoon of butter on low heat—be sure not to burn as they do burn easily. Once they become a little puffy, remove from oil. Add the chicken to this pan and cook on both sides until brown. Set aside.

2 cups long-grain uncooked basmati rice
10 skinless chicken thighs
5 cups of water
1 stick butter
2 cups of plain yogurt
1 large onion, thinly sliced
½ teaspoon saffron dissolved in 1 tablespoon hot water
½ cup dried barberries (zereshk), cleaned, washed and drained
¼ cup slivered toasted almonds
Salt and pepper to taste

In a nonstick pot, add one layer of chicken, one layer of rice, and one layer of the onion/yogurt mixture. Repeat layering until you've used up all ingredients. Put the pot on the stove over medium-high heat for about 30 minutes. When you notice steam, lower the heat, add a dish towel on top of the pot to prevent steam from escaping so it can form a crust and add the lid.

Invert a round platter over the top of the pot and flip it over to drop the Tah-chin onto the platter. Garnish with the sautéed barberry and toasted almonds. This dish is best served with torshi, salad, or tzatziki sauce.

Beef Meqlobe (Upside-Down Rice Dish)

Wash and rinse rice. Transfer it to a nonstick pot and add 5 cups of water and salt to taste. Bring to a boil. Cook until al dente/firm to the bite, about 5–7 minutes. Drain the rice and leave in strainer.

Sauté the chopped onions in oil until golden brown. Add chopped garlic and cardamom. Add the meat and mix until the meat is well combined with the onion and garlic. Add broth, salt, allspice and cinnamon. Cover and allow to cook on medium heat until meat is tender. Check for water; make sure the liquid has not evaporated. When the meat is cooked, remove the pot from the stove and allow to cool. Reserve the liquid from cooking the beef for the end.

In the meantime, wash and squeeze out the liquid off the eggplant to remove all salt and set aside. You will need a Pyrex baking dish. Pour the reserved liquid from the meat onto the bottom of the baking dish. Place one layer of rice on top. Add a layer of eggplant slices flat down into the Pyrex dish, add a layer of the meat (shred it into pieces), another layer of rice, another layer of meat, and finish the top layer with rice.

Cover with aluminum foil and bake in the oven at 350 degrees for 30 minutes. Remove from stove. Garnish with pine nuts, almonds. If adding raisins, heat them in 1 tablespoon oil and sauté until puffy. Add to the top of this dish.

Note: This is another favorite of mine.

2 cups long-grain uncooked basmati rice
2 pounds of beef (I like shank, but cubes for stew meat will also work.)
1 medium eggplant, sliced and salted set aside
1 large onion, chopped
2 large potatoes, peeled and sliced thin
3 cups beef broth
1 teaspoon cinnamon
1 teaspoon seven spice (or allspice)
5 cardamom pods (or 1 teaspoon ground cardamom)
1 bunch fresh cilantro, washed and chopped
¼ cup cooking oil
5 cups water (for rice)
Salt and pepper to taste
¼ cup pine nuts, toasted
¼ cup almonds, toasted
¼ cup yellow raisins (optional)

Kurdish Biryani

Wash and rinse rice. Transfer it to a nonstick pot and add 5 cups of water and salt to taste. Bring to a boil. Cook until al dente/firm to the bite, about 5–7 minutes. Drain the rice and leave in strainer.

Wash and rinse the chicken. Heat a couple of tablespoons of oil. Add the chopped onions until they are golden. Add the chicken and fry on both sides. Add 2 cups of water, Madras curry, turmeric, salt and pepper, and allow the chicken to cook for 15 minutes. Remove the chicken and the onions from the broth and set aside.

Sprinkle the potatoes with salt, pepper, and turmeric. Heat oil on a nonstick pan, fry the potatoes until golden and crunchy, set aside.

In the same pan, fry the almonds until golden in oil, be careful not to burn; add the raisins and the barberries and mix to caramelize. Sauté until the raisins become puffy; set aside.

In the same frying pan, heat a couple more tablespoons of oil; add cut vermicelli and sauté until golden brown. Add the frozen vegetables (carrots and peas) mix until the peas have completely softened.

Combine the cooked rice, potatoes, vegetable, and the vermicelli noodle in a large bowl. Fry one large pita bread or a flour tortilla on both sides, add the cooked chicken, and then add the rice mixture on top. Cover and simmer on low heat for 30 minutes. Remove the lid and place a large round serving plate on top of the pot and turn the chicken and rice upside down onto the serving plate. It will look like a cake, cut the top of the pita bread like a cake, and pour the almonds, raisins, barberries on top.

3 cups long-grain uncooked basmati rice

½ cup vermicelli noodles (can be found at your local stores)

6 skinless chicken thighs

2 large potatoes, cut into small cubes

1 small bag frozen mixed carrots and peas, washed and drained

2 teaspoon Madras curry

2 teaspoon turmeric powder

2 medium onion, chopped

1 cup vegetable oil

6 cups water

1 large flour tortilla or pita bread

1 cup blanched almonds

1 cup dried barberries, washed and rinsed (optional)

1 cup golden raisins

Salt to taste

Red Rice with Chicken

Wash and drain chicken and sear in a nonstick pan over medium-high until golden brown on both sides. Remove the chicken from the pan and set aside.

Sauté the onions in the same pot in some oil until transparent. Add cumin, cardamom, salt and pepper. Put the golden chicken in the pot and pour the diluted tomato paste on top. Bring to boil. Reduce heat to low and cover for 30 minutes.

Strain the chicken from the cooking liquid and place in a baking dish. Pour the cooking liquid in a bowl. In the same pot, add the rice to this mixture, with a teaspoon of salt, the cooking liquid and enough water so that there's half an inch of liquid above the rice. Gently mix. Bring the rice to a boil, reduce to low, and cook covered for 15 minutes. Heat oil in a small frying pan until sizzling. Pour on top of the rice. Cook covered on low for 10 minutes.

In the meantime, reheat the chicken until the skin is crisp. Serve the rice in a platter topped with the chicken pieces.

1 whole chicken cut up (or 1 pound chicken thighs)
2 cups long-grain uncooked basmati rice
1 medium onion, chopped
1 (6 oz.) can tomato paste, diluted in 1 cup water
3 cups hot water
1 teaspoon ground cumin
5 cardamom pods or 1 teaspoon ground cardamom
¼ cup vegetable oil
Salt and pepper to taste

Plain Couscous

Heat oil in a small pot. Add the couscous, salt and pepper. Mix well, until couscous is a little crisp. Add the chicken broth. Bring to a boil, and then reduce heat to low. Cook covered for 10 minutes or until couscous is fluffy and liquid is absorbed.

Serve this as a main dish with salad or torshi. You may use water instead of the chicken broth, although broth is much tastier. Couscous can be found in most grocery stores.

2 cups couscous
3 cups chicken broth
4 tablespoons of vegetable oil
Salt and pepper to taste

Bulgur with Fried Noodles

Bulgur is wheat that has been parboiled, dried, and cracked into nobly bits. It cooks fast and tastes good. Bulgur can be fine or coarse. I prefer to use bulgur no. 2 or no. 3.

Cut the vermicelli noodles in small pieces and sauté in hot oil in a small pot until golden brown. Add the bulgur and mix well. Add the broth or water and a pinch of salt to a boil. Bring to a boil for 5 minutes before reducing the heat and simmering for 5–10 minutes or until tender.

Pour into a platter and garnish the top with roasted almonds and raisins. You can serve this as a main dish with any side dishes, such as soup, salad, or torshi.

2 cups medium-grain bulgur (no. 2 or no. 3)
3 cups chicken broth or water
1 cup vermicelli noodles
1 cup roasted almonds for garnishing
1 cup raisins for garnishing (optional)
¼ cup of vegetable oil

Tomato Sauce Bulgur

In a pot, heat the oil in a saucepan until it is sizzling. Add the bulgur. Mix well. Add broth or water, tomato paste, a pinch of salt and pepper, and bring to a boil. Cover and reduce heat. Simmer for 15–20 minutes or until tender.

You can serve this as a main dish with any side dishes, such as salad or torshi.

Note: You can add mixed vegetables to this dish if desired.

2 cups medium-grain bulgur (no. 2 or no. 3)
3 cups chicken or beef broth, or water
1 (6 oz.) can tomato paste
¼ cup of vegetable oil
Salt and pepper to taste

Vegetarian Barley Soup

Bring water to a boil in a pot. Add the barley, salt, and boil for 1 hour. More water may be needed.

Bring 3 cups water to a boil in a separate pot and add the lentils. Cook over medium heat for 30 minutes or until the lentils are tender.

Clean the spinach, parsley, and cilantro in several changing water to rinse off anything on the leaves. Wash and cut off the root ends of the green onions and coarsely chop all the vegetables and set aside.

Heat oil over medium-high heat. Add chopped onions and sauté. Add the dried mint and mix. Add turmeric, salt and pepper, and dried mint. Cook for 5 minutes. Add to the barley pot.

Add to the barley, the chickpeas, and the pinto beans. Allow to cook on medium to low heat for 1 hour, stirring occasionally to prevent the bottom from sticking to the pot. Taste and adjust the seasoning. Use your judgment for the water. If the soup is thick, you can add water to thin it as you desire. If it the soup is too thin, then allow to simmer by uncovering the lid to allow the liquid to evaporate.

Garnishes: Heat 2 tablespoons of oil and add the dried mint. Sauté for 3–5 minutes or until the color of oil changes to green. Remove and set aside. Pour the soup in a large serving bowl and top with kashk and sautéed mint. Serve with your choice of bread. This is especially comforting in the cold winter.

1 cup barley, washed and drained
1 cup green lentils, washed and drained
1 (15.5 oz.) can chickpeas, rinsed and drained
1 (15.5 oz.) can pinto beans
2 bunches parsley
2 bunches green onion
1 bunches cilantro
½ cup vegetable oil
3 large onions, chopped
2 bunches spinach
1 cup chopped carrots
1 tablespoons dried mint
1 tablespoon turmeric
15 cups water
*2 cups **kashk** (Kashk is a fresh cheese and can be found at Middle Eastern grocery stores.)*

Garnish
Kashk
2 tablespoons dried mint
3 tablespoons oil

Mung Beans Soup

Wash the mung beans, rinse, and then put in a deep pot. Add 3 cups of boiling water and a pinch of salt and let it cook for 20 minutes. Drain and return the mung beans to the pot. Add remaining water and bring to a boil. Add squash; bring to a boil and let it cook on medium-high for 15 minutes.

Heat olive oil in a skillet, add garlic, and cook until golden. Add onions and cook until soft. Add mint. Mix well and pour this in the pot with the mung beans and squash. Bring to a boil. Add the tomato paste, citric acid (or lemon juice), salt and pepper, and let it cook for 10 minutes on medium-high heat. Let it all cook until done.

Pour the bean soup into a large dish and garnish with parsley. You can serve this with any kind of bread and sabzi (green vegetables) on the side.

2 cups mung beans
10 cups water
2 cloves of garlic, chopped
1 winter squash, washed and cut in small cubes
1 large onion, chopped
1 tablespoon dry mint
1 (6 oz.) can of tomato paste
1 teaspoon citric acid (or ½ cup lemon juice)
½ cup olive oil
1 bunch parsley, washed and chopped (garnishing)
Salt and pepper to taste

Noodle Pottage (Ash-e Reshteh)

Heat the olive oil in pot, sauté the onions and garlic. Add dried Ash-e Reshteh, turmeric, salt and pepper. Mix well. Add 6 cups of water and let it boil on a medium heat for 20 minutes. Add cooked lentils, chickpeas, and kidney beans. Bring to a boil. Boil for 30 minutes on medium-high heat. Adjust seasoning if needed. Add the noodles. Bring to boil and let simmer on medium-heat for 30 minutes.

Place some oil in a skillet and add half the kashk (see explanation below). Mix well until the kashk is melted, then add half a cup of dried mint, and mix well until it has soaked up the oil. Add some juice from the Ash-e Reshteh (spaghetti noodles) that is already cooking and stir well. Pour this over the soup mix and continue to let it cook.

In a separate skillet, heat some more oil and add the last part of the kashk and dried mint. Take four tablespoons of the juice from the vegetables that you already cooked and add it to the kashk and the mint. Set aside. Add the remaining garlic and let it sauté until brown. When the Ash-e is cooked and ready to be served, you can pour it into a bowl and garnish with the sautéed mint, garlic, and kashk.

Kashk is made from drained yogurt. Kashk can be found in powder form or liquid. It is similar to whey, which is a dairy product. It is similar to sour cream, and it is used in traditional Kurdish and Iranian cooking. If you use the powder form, then it needs to be soaked and softened before you can use it in cooking.

2 cups dried Ash-e Reshteh vegetable soaked in warm water for two hours prior to cooking
2 tablespoons turmeric
1 cup cooked and drained green lentils
1 (15.5 oz.) can chickpeas
1 (15.5 oz.) can dark red kidney beans
1 large onion, chopped
1 jar of whey (Kashk is available at any Middle Eastern grocery store; see explanation below)
1 cup dry mint
1 cup olive oil
½ package noodles for Ash (Similar to spaghetti noodles; you can find at any Middle Eastern markets)
½ cup garlic, chopped (divide in half portions)
12 cups water
Salt and pepper to taste

Broccoli Soup

Pour the vegetable stock into a large saucepan and bring to a boil. Add chopped broccoli. Allow to cook over medium heat for 15 minutes.

After the broccoli has cooked slightly and it is soft enough, you can puree it with an electric hand blender until smooth. Add skim milk to the mixture. Cover and cook on low heat for 10 minutes. Pour into a large bowl and garnish with cheddar cheese. Serve with toasted pita bread or your choice of crackers.

3 cups chopped broccoli (about one large bunch)
2 cups vegetable stock
½ cup cheddar cheese
1 cup skim milk
¼ cup finely chopped red onion

Chickpeas and Beef Stew

Wash and rinse beef, put it in a pot, and sauté until dry. Add 5 cups of water and let it boil until the meat is tender, about 15 minutes. Wash the dried limes and poke each with holes using the tip of a knife. Add to the meat and let boil for 15 minutes.

Heat the oil, sauté onions until soft; add crushed tomato, turmeric, salt and pepper, and the diluted tomato paste. Mix well and pour over the beef. Allow to cook for 30 minutes. Serve with rice or bread.

1 pound lean beef cut in cubes (You can use any part, but I like cubes.)
2 (15.5 oz.) cans chickpeas, rinsed and drained
1 can diced or crushed tomatoes
2 tablespoon tomatoes paste diluted in 1 cup boiled hot water
*2 dried limes (**limo amman**) or fresh lemon juice*
1 large onion, quartered
1 teaspoon turmeric
¼ cup vegetable oil
5 cups of water
Salt and pepper to taste

Chickpeas and Chicken Stew

Wash and rinse the chicken. Season with salt and set aside. Brown the chicken in a pot until dry. Add oil, onions, garlic, cumin, turmeric, crushed pepper, salt/pepper, and lemon juice. Bring to a boil, cover, and let cook for 20 minutes.

Add the chickpeas and remaining water. Cover and let cook for 15–20 more minutes. Add more water if needed.

Serve over rice or just with plain bread.

6 skinless chicken thighs
2 cans (15.5 oz.) chickpeas, drained
1 large onion, chopped
3 large cloves garlic, minced
1 tablespoon ground cumin
1 teaspoon turmeric
1 teaspoon crushed red pepper flakes
1 teaspoon black pepper
4 cups of water
1 freshly squeezed lemon
½ cup olive oil (divided into 2 equal parts)
Salt and pepper to taste

Green Bean and Meat Stew

Sauté the meat in oil until it is browned. Add onion and cook for 15 minutes.

In a separate pot, boil the green beans for about 10 minutes. Drain. Add to the meat mixture. Add crushed tomatoes, tomato paste, salt and pepper; mix well. Cook for 30 minutes on low-medium heat or until the green beans are soft and meat is tender.

Serve with rice.

1 pound beef or lamb cut into cubes
1 large onion, finely chopped
1 pound green beans, cut into 1-inch pieces
1 can crushed tomatoes
¼ cup tomato paste
1½ cups water (or more if too dry)
3 tablespoons vegetable oil
Salt and pepper to taste

Yellow Lentil Soup

Wash and rinse lentils and put in a pot with 3 cups of water. Allow to cook on medium-high heat until the lentils are smooth. Reduce heat to low. Mix occasionally. Add the chicken broth. Let it cook for 15 minutes longer.

In a separate pan, melt the butter and sauté onions until golden brown. Add to the lentil soup while it is still cooking. Also, add the frozen peas and carrots, garlic powder, salt, pepper, turmeric, dill, and lemon juice. Cook for another 30 minutes. Taste to adjust seasoning. If the soup is too thick, you may add more broth or just boiled water.

Remove from heat and pour in a large bowl and serve with French or pita bread.

2 cups yellow lentils
3 cups water
6 cups chicken broth
1 medium onion, finely chopped
1 stick butter or margarine
1 tablespoon turmeric
1 tablespoon dill
1 teaspoon garlic powder
½ cup frozen peas (optional)
½ cup frozen carrots (optional)
4 tablespoon lemon juice or fresh cut lemons
Salt and pepper to taste

Celery Beef Stew

Wash and drain the meat. In a pot, brown the meat until almost dry, then add oil, onion, turmeric, salt, pepper, and water; cook for 35 minutes or until the meat is tender.

Melt the butter in a saucepan; add celery and sauté until the celery is soft. Add in the parsley, mint, dried limes, and lemon juice to the mixture. Cook for 3–5 minutes then add to the meat mixture. Allow to simmer for another 20–30 minutes.

Serve over rice or with your choice of bread.

1 pound lean beef cut in cubes
1 head of celery, washed and cut into 2-inch pieces
1 large onion, finely chopped
1 bunch fresh parsley, chopped
1 tablespoon dried mint
1 teaspoon turmeric
4 dried limes (or dried lemon powder)
1 tablespoon lemon juice
1 stick butter
Salt and pepper to taste

Eggplant Casserole (Tapsi)

Cut the eggplants in ½-inch round slices and sprinkle both sides of each slice lightly with salt. Wash the meat, then sauté in a pot until brown and dry. Add water, salt, pepper, and bring to boil for 20–30 minutes.

In a skillet, sauté onion in oil until golden brown. Remove the onion and set aside. Drain the excess water from the eggplant. Add the eggplant to the same oil used for the onions and fry both sides. Remove eggplant from the skillet.

In a Pyrex baking dish, add one layer of eggplant, top with a layer of onion, layer of tomatoes, and layer of meat. Pour dissolved tomato paste over the dish. Cover with aluminum foil and put in the oven at 350 degrees for 15–20 minutes. Serve with rice.

1 pound lean beef stew meat cut in 1-inch pieces
3 medium eggplants
3 large tomatoes, halved and sliced
1 large onion, halved and sliced
2 tablespoons tomato paste dissolved in ½ cup hot water
½ cup vegetable oil
Salt and pepper to taste

Stuffed Eggplant (Sheikh Mahshi)

Cut the eggplants in half and core/scoop the inside with a small knife to create a cone shape with a hollow inside. Sprinkle salt all over to soften them. Set aside while you prepare the filling.

In a skillet, sauté the meat until it is almost dry. Then, add oil, onions, mint, salt and pepper. Stir well until onions are limp and meat is brown. Add chopped parsley and mix well. Drain this meat mixture in a colander to remove excess liquid.

Rinse the salt off the eggplants. Put a tablespoon of the filling into each half of the cone-shaped eggplant. Put the two parts of the eggplant back together. You can wrap the two eggplants with a long stem of parsley to prevent from opening up while baking, or you can just put them together. Continue this process until you have stuffed all the eggplants.

Gently place the eggplants on the bottom of a Pyrex baking dish. You should have 1 layer of eggplant in the dish only. If any of the meat mixture is left, you can sprinkle on top of the eggplants. Pour the diluted tomato paste over the eggplant. Cover with aluminum foil and bake for 30 minutes at 350 degrees. Gently remove with a spatula and put onto a platter or you can leave in the baking dish. Serve with rice.

This is a popular Kurdish dish.

6 large, long, and straight Italian eggplants or zucchini or both (I used eggplant)
1 pound lean ground beef
2 tablespoons dry mint
1 bunch fresh parsley, chopped
1 large onion, chopped
1 (6 oz.) can tomato paste, dissolved in ½ cup hot water
¼ cup vegetable oil
Salt and pepper to taste

Persian Herb Stew (Ghormeh Sabzi)

Wash the beef and add to a pot with water. Bring to a boil. Poke the dried limes with the tip of the knife, putting a few holes in it to allow the juice to enter. Add the limes to the pot. Boil for 30 minutes or until meat is tender.

In a separate large pot, heat oil in a pot and sauté onion until translucent. Add the dried Ghormeh Sabzi herbs and mix until well coated with oil. Add turmeric, salt and pepper. Pour the beef and limes, along with any remaining liquid over the herbs. Allow to boil for 30 minutes on medium heat.

Add the kidney beans. Cook on medium heat for 20 minutes, covered. Continue to stir often to prevent from drying out. Add water as needed and adjust the seasoning to your liking (more salt/pepper/lemon juice).

Serve over white rice.

Note: This dish is a popular Iranian dish. Since I lived in Iran, I am a big fan of this dish. I make it all the time.

1 can/bag dried Ghormeh Sabzi herbs (found at any Middle Eastern groceries)

1½ pounds beef cut in cubes (preferably neck bones)

5 dried limes

1 medium onion

1 teaspoon turmeric

2 (15.5 oz.) cans dark red kidney beans

1 tablespoon tomato paste (optional)

½ cup of vegetable oil

1 tablespoon lemon juice

6 cups water

Salt and pepper to taste

White Bean and Meat Stew

Wash the meat. Heat oil in a small pot and add the meat. Cook until the meat is browned. Add 6 cups of water, salt, pepper and bring to a boil for 30 minutes or until meat is tender.

In a separate small pan, heat oil and sauté onions until translucent. Add tomato paste and mix well. Add crushed tomatoes and season with salt/pepper to taste. Add to the meat mixture. Continue to boil for 15–20 minutes, covered.

Serve with rice.

Note: This dish is normally made in the winter.

*1 pound of beef or lamb cut into 1-inch cubes
(or use neck bones)*
6 cups water
*2 (15.5 oz.) cans white kidney beans (or use
dry beans but soak overnight)*
1 medium onion, finely chopped
*1 can crushed tomatoes (16 oz.) or use fresh
tomatoes, finely chopped*
cup vegetable oil
1 (6 oz.) can tomato paste
Salt and pepper to taste

Potato and Meat Stew

Wash the meat. Heat oil in a small pot and add the meat. Cook until the meat is browned. Add 4 cups of water, salt, pepper and bring to a boil for 30 minutes or until meat is tender. Add the diluted tomato paste.

In a medium pot, heat oil and sauté the onion until translucent. Add the potatoes and turmeric; mix well until well coated. Add the meat and its liquid to the pot. Bring to a boil and allow to cook for 15–20 minutes, covered on low heat.

Serve over rice.

1 pound beef or lamb, cut into
1-inch pieces
4 large potatoes, peeled and cubed
1 (6 oz.) can tomato paste diluted
in 1 cup boiled water
1 medium onion, sliced
3 tablespoons lemon juice or ½ tsp
citric acid
4 cups water
1 teaspoon turmeric
¼ cup vegetable oil
Salt and pepper to taste

Kurdish Lamb Shanks

Wash and rinse the shanks. Season with salt and pepper. Heat one cup olive oil in a nonstick pan, and brown the shanks on all sides. Add 5 cups of water and bring to boil on medium heat for 1 hour.

Add the onions, celery, carrots, and garlic to the shanks. Mix well. Add curry, turmeric, rosemary, thyme, dried limes, salt and pepper to taste. Cook for 1–2 hours on low heat. You may add more water if needed. Make sure the liquid is above the shanks in order for them to cook well. They must be very tender before serving.

Once the shanks are tender, transfer it to a platter. Serve it with plain rice or bread.

6–8 lamb shanks

5 dried limes (Note: This can be found at any Mediterranean supermarket.)

3 tablespoons dried rosemary

3 carrots, peeled and cut into ½-inch pieces

1 cup celery, chopped

2 tablespoons curry powder

2 tablespoons turmeric

2 tablespoons thyme

1 large onion, chopped

5 cloves garlic

5 cups water

1 cup olive oil

Salt and pepper to taste

Okra and Beef Stew

Wash the meat. Place in a medium pot. Add 5 cups water. Bring to a boil. Add the tomato paste and mix well. Allow to boil for 30 minutes, covered, until meat is tender.

In a separate pot, sauté garlic in oil until brown; add okra. Mix well until okra is well coated in oil and garlic. Add tomatoes, lemon juice, salt and pepper; mix well. Add the meat and its liquid to this mixture. Bring to a boil; reduce to medium heat and cook for 30 minutes until okra is soft, but not slimy. Serve over rice.

1½ pounds beef, cut into 1-inch pieces or use neck bones
2 medium tomatoes, chopped
2 large cloves garlic, chopped
1 (6 oz.) can tomato paste
1 pound fresh okra, tops trimmed (or 1 bag frozen whole okra)
¼ cup lemon juice
¼ cup oil
5 cups water
Salt and pepper to taste

Spinach Stew

Wash the meat. Place in a medium pot. Add 5 cups water. Bring to a boil. Add the tomato paste and mix well. Allow to boil for 30 minutes, covered, until meat is tender.

Heat oil in a medium pot. Add onion and sauté until translucent. Add spinach, parsley, turmeric, salt and pepper. Mix well. Pour the meat stew into this mixture and add the lemon juice. Adjust salt/pepper to your desired taste. Stir and simmer for an additional 15–20 minutes.

Serve over rice, bread, or crackers.

2 bunch fresh spinach, washed and chopped
(or use 1 large bag frozen spinach)
1 pound beef cut in 1-inch cubes
1 bunch parsley, chopped
1 large onion, chopped
1 (6 oz.) can tomato paste
½ cup lemon juice
2 teaspoons turmeric
¼ cup oil
5 cups water
Salt and pepper to taste

Vegetable Soup

Heat the oil in a large and deep pot; add onion and sauté until a golden. Add garlic and sauté until brown. Add all of the vegetables (celery, potatoes, carrots, and parsley) mix well. Add vegetable stock, tomato paste, turmeric, coriander, lemon juice, salt and pepper to taste. Bring to a boil. Add the beans. Bring to another boil. Cover, reduce the heat, and allow it to cook for 35–45 minutes on medium heat. Adjust seasoning and add more liquid if needed. Serve hot with crackers or bread.

Note: This is a hearty, winter dish. It's very filling.

2 large potatoes, diced
1 cup fresh spinach, finely chopped (or 1 bag frozen)
1 large onion, finely chopped
1 clove garlic minced
1 cup carrots chopped
1 bunch fresh parsley, chopped
1 cup celery chopped
1 (6 oz.) can tomato paste
1 (15.5 oz.) can red kidney beans, drained
1 (15.5 oz.) can white pinto beans (washed and rinsed
1 tablespoon coriander
1 tablespoon turmeric
 cup oil
10 cups of water or vegetable stock
Salt and pepper to taste

Split Peas and Beef Stew

Melt the butter in a nonstick pan over medium-high heat and add onions; fry until golden brown. Wash the meat and add to the onions, increase heat to high. Fry until all juices evaporate, about 5 minutes. Add tomato paste, salt, pepper, and turmeric, then mix well. Fry for 5–10 minutes until tomato paste changes the color of oil to red. Add 3 cups of water to the mixture cover and bring to boil on medium low heat. Cook for 1 hour.

While the meat is cooking, wash and boil the split peas in 2 cups of water in a medium size saucepan until the split peas are tender, drain and set aside.

Check the meat and once it is tender, add the split peas and dried lime powder; cook for 30 minutes on medium heat, covered. You can taste and adjust the seasoning as needed.

Heat the ½ cup of oil in a large frying pan. Add the potatoes and cook until golden brown. Remove the potatoes from the oil and onto a paper towel to drain any excess oil.

Pour the stew into a large serving bowl. Top with fries just before serving. This is great with bread or rice.

1 pound lean beef, cut into 1 inch cubes
1 cup yellow split peas, picked over, rinsed and drained
2 large potatoes peeled and cut lengthwise, similar to french fries
1 large onion, chopped
2 tablespoon tomato paste
1 tablespoon dried lime powder
½ teaspoon turmeric
5 cups water
1 stick butter
½ cup oil
Salt and pepper to taste

Walnut Stew (Fesinjon)

Brown the walnuts in butter or oil on low heat. Stir constantly to prevent from burning. Remove the walnuts from the oil and set aside.

Sauté the onions lightly in the same butter or oil until translucent. Remove the onions with a spoon. Brown the chicken on both sides in the same pan; add sugar, cinnamon, and pomegranate syrup; mix well. Let simmer on low heat for 10 minutes. Add the walnuts and onions to the chicken. Add water. Bring to a boil, and then reduce heat to medium and cover. Allow to boil for 1 hour. Adjust salt as needed. Stir occasionally to prevent sticking. Serve over plain rice.

1 pound skinless chicken cut in serving-size pieces

2 medium onions, chopped

3 cups walnuts, finely ground

3 tablespoons lemon juice

3 tablespoons sugar

½ teaspoon cinnamon

¼ cup of pomegranate syrup (found in Middle Eastern groceries)

¼ cup vegetable oil or butter

5 cups water

Note: This is an Iranian dish shared by a dear Iranian friend.

Zucchini and Beef Stew

Wash meat and drain. Put the meat into a nonstick pot and cook until the meat is dry (liquid has evaporated). Add oil and sauté the onions until translucent. Add water and bring to a boil. Cover and reduce heat to medium and cook until meat is tender, about 30 minutes. Add tomato paste and mix until well dissolved in the water. Add the zucchini, turmeric, salt and pepper. Mix and let simmer over low heat for 15–20 minutes. Serve over rice.

1 pound lean beef (cut into 1-inch cubes)
4–6 zucchini, cubed
1 medium onion, sliced
1 teaspoon turmeric
1 (6 oz.) can tomato paste
¼ cup vegetable oil
2 cups of water
Salt and pepper to taste

Kofteh in Tomato Sauce (Tirkshik)

Filling: In a large skillet or pot, brown the meat. Add chopped onion and mix for about 5 minutes. Add chopped parsley, salt and pepper to taste. Place the meat in a colander to drain excess liquid. Set aside to cool.

Dough: Mix the cream of rice and the cream of wheat in a large bowl. Add ground beef and mix until well combined. Add water, salt and pepper to form dough. Mix until soft, but do not let it get too watery or it will not stick together.

Assembling: Once the dough is ready, shape the dough into golf ball–sized portions. With your thumb, press a hole in the middle of the ball for the filling. The sides of the ball should be thin; remember that the dough will expand in the soup while cooking too. *Note:* I like to dip my hands in a bowl of water to keep the dough from sticking to my hands while stuffing the dough balls. Fill each dough/shell with a tablespoon of meat filling. Use same amount of filling for each kofteh by using a tablespoon to maintain this measurement. Close the dough together and flatten slightly like a pancake. Add the finished kofteh to a tray. Repeat the process until the dough is finished. If there is any remaining meat mixture you can add to the soup later.

Soup: Heat oil, sauté onion until golden brown. Add the celery and cook until the celery is soft. Add the spinach or the Swiss chard until wilted. Add 12 cups of water and bring to boil. Add the tomato paste, salt, pepper, and lemon juice or citric acid to taste. Allow the vegetables to cook on medium heat for 15 minutes. Reduce the heat. Drop each kofteh slowly into the soup while the soup is boiling; gently stir from the side with a flat spoon to ensure the kofteh is not stuck to the bottom of the pot. If you see the soup is thick and not enough to cook the kofteh in, then you can add some more boiled water. Allow for the kofteh to cook for about 30 minutes or until the kofteh begins to float. Turn off the heat. Remove each kofteh with a spatula or slotted spoon and put onto a platter. Pour the soup on a separate bowl and serve.

Note: This dish is time consuming, but it is delicious. I make it once a month for my family.

Filling
2 pounds ground beef (lean and uncooked)
1 large onion, chopped
1 bunch parsley, washed and chopped
Salt and pepper to taste

Dough
2 cups cream of rice
2 cups of water (may need more)
1 cup cream of wheat (uncooked)
½ pound lean ground beef
Salt and pepper to taste

Soup
*12 cups of water (**Note:** It may need more depending on how thick it becomes when cooking the kofteh.)*
2 bunches fresh spinach or Swiss chard, washed and chopped coarsely
1 bunch celery, washed and chopped
1 (6 oz.) can of tomato paste
½ cup vegetable oil
½ cup lemon juice (You can use more if needed after you taste it.)
Salt and paper to taste

Kofteh in Yogurt Sauce (Dooghavah)

Filling: In a large skillet or pot, brown the meat. Add chopped onion and mix for about 5 minutes. Add chopped parsley, salt and pepper to taste. Place the meat in a colander to drain excess liquid. Set aside to cool.

Dough: Mix the cream of rice and the cream of wheat in a large bowl. Add ground beef and mix until well combined. Add water, salt and pepper to form dough. Mix until soft, but do not let it get too watery or it will not stick together.

Assembling: Once it is ready, shape the dough into golf ball–sized portions. With your thumb, press a hole in the middle of the ball for stuffing. The sides of the ball should be thin; remember that the dough will expand in the soup while cooking too. *Note:* I like to dip my hands in a bowl of water to keep the dough from sticking to my hands while stuffing the dough balls. This dish is similar to tirkshik above. Fill each dough ball (or shell) with the cooled cooked meat using about the same amount per ball, or use a spoon to maintain the stuffing measurements. Close together and pat. Flatten the stuffed kofteh into discs and put them on a baking pan. After all the balls have been stuffed, they are ready to go into the soup.

Soup: In a large nonstick pot, mix the yogurt and water together well. Mix continuously over medium-high heat and bring to a boil. Once it comes to a boil, add the eggs to the mixture and continue the mixing until smooth. (The eggs prevent the yogurt from curdling). Allow this mix to cook on low heat for about 20 minutes. Add the chickpeas and dried oregano to the soup. Let it cook for 10 minutes. Carefully drop in the kofteh that you prepared. Mix gently. Cook for 25 additional minutes on medium heat or until the kofteh floats. When serving, remove the kofteh with a draining spoon and put them on a platter. Pour the soup in a separate dish and serve together.

Dough

2 cups cream of rice
2 cups of water (may need more)
1 cup cream of wheat (it should be uncooked)
1 pound ground beef (lean and uncooked)
Salt and pepper to taste

Filling

2 pounds ground beef (lean and uncooked)
1 large onion, chopped
1 bunch parsley, washed and chopped
Salt and pepper to taste

Soup

6 cups of plain yogurt (store-bought or homemade)
1 large can of chickpeas, rinsed and drained
½ cup of dried oregano
2 eggs, beaten
Salt and pepper to taste
Water (you may need to add more boiling water in the process, depending on how thick it becomes when cooking the kofteh)

Stuffed Peppers

Heat half the oil and sauté onion until translucent. Add garlic and stir for 1 minute. Add the ground beef and let it cook over medium-high heat until thoroughly brown. Add parsley, coriander, salt and pepper, and cook for 5–7 minutes.

In a pot, add water, rice, salt and remaining oil; mix well and bring to a boil. Cover and reduce heat to low for 10–15 minutes. Remove the rice from this pot and place in a large bowl.

Add the meat to the rice. Stuff each pepper with the rice/meat mixture. Place the top of the pepper back onto the pepper. Lay the stuffed bell peppers into a casserole (Pyrex) dish, and pour the diluted tomato sauce over the bell peppers. Cover with aluminum foil and bake at 400 degrees for 10–15 minutes. Serve as a main course.

6 bell peppers (any color—red, green or yellow; cut top off and reserve; remove the insides)
1 pound ground beef
1 cup onion, chopped
1 bunch fresh parsley, chopped
1 clove garlic, minced
1 teaspoon ground coriander
1 cup white rice (washed and rinsed)
1 (6 oz.) can tomato paste diluted in one cup hot water
1½ cup water
¼ cup oil
Salt and pepper to taste

Stuffed Vegetable (Dolma)

Wash rice and rinse; in a large bowl, add chopped meat, tomato paste, parsley, onions, garlic, ½ cup oil, salt and pepper, lemon juice or citric acid to taste. Mix well and set aside.

I normally put ribs or chicken in the bottom of the pot that I make the dolma in. Brown both sides of your choice of meat and leave in the pot.

Cut the stem of the cabbage. Peel off the leaves and blanch in large pot of boiling water. Allow to boil until leaves are softened, but not too soft. Remove the leaves with a slotted spoon.

Place a tablespoon of the rice mixture onto 1 cabbage leaf and roll. Place in the pot (on top of the meat if you are using meat at the bottom of the pot). Continue rolling the cabbage leaves and placing in the pot until you have one layer.

Next take a tablespoon of the rice mixture onto each grape leaf and roll. Add on top of the cabbage layer in the pot. Finish until you have made one layer in the pot.

Take a tablespoon of the rice mixture and add to a layer of the onion. Roll and place on top of the grape leaves in the pot. Continue until you've finished the layers of onions.

Stuff the eggplants with the rice mixture. Place on top of the onions in the pot. Next, stuff the zucchini and the tomatoes. If you have leftover rice mixture, you can add another layer of the stuffed grape leaves or cabbage leaves. Be sure the top layer is some stuffed grape leaves or cabbage.

Place the pot onto the stove over medium-high heat. Add the remaining oil. Pour 2 cups boiling water on top. Put a flat, heavy plate on top of the vegetables to keep them from opening during the cooking process. Boil for 15 minutes. Taste the water after a few minutes of boiling. If you need to adjust the salt or lemon juice, you can do so.

4 cups uncooked short-grain rice such as Jasmine

1 pound chuck beef or lamb, finely chopped, washed and rinsed

1 jar grape leaves (remove from jar and pour hot water over to rinse off the excess salt)

1 small head cabbage (prefer Chinese because the leaves are softer)

2 onions (makes about six once the leaves are separated)

2 eggplants (skinny Italian, cut in half and core each one)

2 zucchini (choose the long ones, cut in half and core each one)

2 round tomatoes (cut the top and core inside)

1 cup olive oil (or vegetable oil)

4 cloves garlic, chopped

1 (6 oz.) small can tomato paste

1 bunch of fresh parsley, finely chopped

1 small onion finely chopped

1 cup lemon juice (or 1 tablespoon citric acid)

Salt and pepper to taste

3 cups water (you may need to use more to cook through)

½ pound beef ribs or skinless chicken thighs (optional to use in the bottom of the pot)

Reduce heat to low and allow to cook for another 20 minutes. While cooking, use the end of a fork and poke the edge of the leaves so that excess water goes downward rather than staying on top of the stuffed vegetable. Make sure you don't tear the stuffed vegetable during this process. Cook until all the water is gone. Also, check to see if the rice is cooked. If not, add more water until the rice is ready. When cooking is complete, flip the pot upside down onto large platter. This dish is ready to serve.

Note: This dish is common in the Middle East. Everyone makes it slightly different. This is one of my favorite dishes that I make frequently.

Rice-and-Dill-Stuffed Grape Leaves (Dolma)

Remove the grape leaves from the jar and remove the stems. Rinse the leaves in several changing water and set aside.

If using meat, wash and rinse first; then sprinkle with some salt and pepper and cook in a nonstick pot that you will place the dolma into. Sauté the meat until it's dry. Add ½ cup oil to the meat and cook until browned on both sides. Leave in the pot; the grape leaves will be added on top.
Wash and rinse rice, add dill, garlic, onions, yogurt, ½ cup oil, citric acid, salt and pepper; mix well. Now you are ready to stuff the leaves.

Place a tablespoon of filling in the bottom center of the leaf, just above the stem. Fold the bottom section up to cover the filling. Fold the sides in toward the center. Keep on rolling the leaves up toward the top point of the leaf. Place the rolls in layers in the pan over the meat. Be sure to place the leaves with the seam on the bottom to prevent from opening.

3 cups of uncooked short grain rice, such as Jasmine
2 bunch green onions, chopped
4 cloves of garlic, minced
3 bunch fresh dill, washed and chopped
1 tablespoon dried mint
1½ cup olive oil
1 cup plain yogurt
1 tablespoon citric acid
1 cup lemon juice (or boil ½ cup whole sumac then strain and use the juice)
6 chicken thighs or beef/lamb ribs for the bottom of the pot
1½ cups water (may need more)
Salt and black pepper to taste

Stuff all the leaves, and if you have leftover rice, then you can use more leaves. If you have leftover leaves and no rice, you can put the leaves in a Ziploc and freeze them for the next time you make dolma.
Pour the remaining half cup of oil over the stuffed leaves. Add the sumac or lemon juice and enough water to come over the grape leaves by about an inch. Place an inverted heavy plate on top of the leaves to prevent them from opening and keep them submerged in the water.

Taste some of the excess juice in order to determine if you need to add more salt or lemon juice. You can adjust the seasoning while there is still water in the pot. Let cook on medium-high for 10 minutes. While cooking, use the end of the fork and poke the edge of the leaves so that excess water goes downward rather than staying on top of the leaves. Make sure you don't tear the leaves during this process. Check to see if the rice is tender after 15 minutes. If so, then take the plate off the leaves. If rice is still firm, add more water and put the lid back on; allow to simmer for 10 minutes on low heat.

When cooking is complete, put a flat platter that is big enough to cover the top of the pot and turn the pot upside down onto the platter. This dish is ready to serve.

Beef Shish Kabob

Mix onion juice and seasonings in a bowl. Add the meat. Cover the meat completely with the mixture. Allow to marinate for 2–3 hours in the refrigerator or overnight. Remove meat from the marinade and place five to six pieces onto a skewer. Broil or grill the meat, turning it frequently and sprinkling simultaneously with crushed sumac. Serve with flatbread or over rice.

1 pound lamb or beef with
* some fat, cut in 1½-inch*
* cubes*
1 teaspoon turmeric
½ teaspoon salt
¼ teaspoon pepper
¼ cup olive oil
Juice of 1 onion
Sumac (optional)

Chicken Tikka

Wash and rinse the chicken and toss it in a bowl. Add garlic, salt, paprika, yogurt, and olive oil and mix well. Cover and marinate for a few hours in the refrigerator.

When ready to grill, pierce a piece of chicken, onion, green pepper, tomato onto a skewer and repeat this process until you've finished all ingredients. Grill the chicken on both sides for about 5–6 minutes. You can brush the excess marinade on the chicken as you grill to keep them moist. Serve with bread, salad, and/or rice.

1 pound of chicken breast, boneless, cut in cube size
2 large tomatoes, cut in cubes (or you can use cherry tomatoes, whole)
1 large onion, quartered
1 large green pepper, quartered
1 clove garlic, minced
½ cup plain yogurt
¾ cups olive oil
½ teaspoon paprika
½ teaspoon red hot pepper
Salt and pepper to taste

Orange-Flavored Baked Chicken

Wash and rinse the chicken, sprinkle with salt and pepper, olive oil, orange peel, minced garlic, and the diluted saffron in a large bowl; mix well. Cover and refrigerate for 30 minutes before cooking.

Remove the chicken from the marinade and place in a well-greased baking dish. Add the potatoes to the marinade and mix well. Immediately remove the potatoes and add on top of the chicken. Layer with the tomatoes on top. Cover with aluminum foil and bake for 25–30 minutes at 350 degrees.
Remove the foil; using a spoon or a turkey baster, remove the liquid from the chicken and pour over the top to prevent from drying. Allow to cook uncovered for an additional 7–10 minutes so the top becomes golden brown. Remove from the oven and let it rest for 5 minutes before serving.
This is an easy and delicious dish that can be served as an entrée.

6 pieces skinless chicken thighs
4 large potatoes, peeled and quartered (place in bowl of cold water until ready to use)
1 large tomato, quartered
2 cloves of garlic, peeled and minced
¼ cup lemon juice (or fresh squeezed lemon)
1 medium orange peel (not the fruit itself, just the peel)
½ teaspoon saffron (dissolved in 2 tablespoon of boiling water)
¼ cup olive oil
Salt and pepper to taste

Kurd Burgers (Shifte)

In a large bowl, combine ground beef, onion, garlic, bread crumbs or flour, parsley, turmeric, salt and pepper to taste. Mix the ingredients well. Ensure the mixture is well formed so that it holds together. If the mixture is too soft, add more bread crumbs or flour. If it is too dry, add water.

Form the meat mixture into oval patties, have a small bowl of cold water available to wet your hands so that the mixture does not stick to your hands. Once all the patties are formed, set aside.

Next, heat the oil in a nonstick pan until sizzling hot. Reduce heat to medium and add the meat patties one at a time until you have filled the pan. Poke each one with a fork to let the steam out and to cook on the inside. Make sure to flip each one so they brown on both sides. Place a paper towel on a plate. Remove the patties from the oil and set them onto the paper towel to absorb any extra oil. *Note:* You may have to reduce heat so as not to burn the patties.

This dish is best with soup, salad, or pita bread.

Note: You can cut a piece of pita bread in half; add a few patties and your choice of greens, tomatoes, onions, and tzatziki sauce. This makes a great sandwich.

2 pounds lean ground beef
2 cloves garlic, minced
1 medium onion, grated
1 bunch fresh parsley, finely chopped
1 cup seasoned bread crumbs or white flour
1 teaspoon turmeric
2 cups vegetable or canola oil
Water
Salt and pepper to taste

Roasted Potatoes and Broccoli

In a skillet, melt the butter and add minced garlic; cook until golden brown. Add the diluted cream of chicken and mix well. Add thyme, salt and pepper to taste.

Wash the broccoli. Put it into a bowl of boiled water and set aside. This will soften the broccoli but not cook it. The next three steps are a series of layering to create the casserole.

In a bowl, place the potatoes and add salt and pepper; mix well. Set aside.

In a greased Pyrex baking dish, add a layer of potatoes, 1 cup of cheese, and drained broccoli. Add another cup of cheese, top with potatoes. Pour cream of chicken mixture over the potatoes. Cover and bake for 1 hour at 350 degrees. Bring the casserole to the table and serve with a salad.

6 large potatoes, peeled and sliced
4 cloves garlic, minced
1 pound fresh broccoli florets (or 1 package frozen broccoli florets)
2 cups shredded cheddar cheese
1 (14 oz.) can cream of chicken, diluted in ½ cup water
1 teaspoon dried thyme
½ stick butter
Salt and pepper to taste

Chuck Roast

First, preheat the oven to 350 degrees. Wash the meat and place in a large bowl. Add salt, pepper, turmeric, paprika, olive oil, yogurt, and garlic. Add the bay leaves to the bottom of a Pyrex baking dish. Lay the roast on top. Cover with aluminum foil and let it cook in the oven for 1 hour in its juices. After 1 hour, check the chuck roast by sticking a sharp knife into it to see if it is cooked all the way through. Add a little bit of beef broth or water. Allow it to cook more as needed.

If you are satisfied with how the meat is cooked, then add the potatoes and carrots. Cover again and bake for another hour. Remove the roast from the oven and allow to rest for 10 minutes before slicing. Place the roast on a platter. Remove the potatoes and the carrots and arrange around the roast on the platter. Pour the remaining juice over the roast.

Serve with salad.

4 pounds boneless chuck roast
4 large potatoes, peeled and quartered
4 large carrots, peeled and chopped (You can use baby carrots.)
3 bay leaves
2 cloves garlic, minced
1 large onion, quartered
1 teaspoon paprika
1 teaspoon turmeric
2 tablespoons plain yogurt
1 cup olive oil
1 cup water or beef broth
Salt and pepper to taste

Beef Liver

Add liver to a pan and sauté until dry (liquid is evaporated). Add lemon juice and mix. Add oil to the pan and sauté for a few minutes on medium-high heat. Add the onions, water, turmeric, salt and pepper. Cover and let simmer over medium heat for 20–30 minutes.

Serve over rice, pita bread, or a salad.

Note: You can cut a piece of pita bread in half; add a few patties and your choice of greens, tomatoes, and pickles/torshi. This makes a great sandwich.

2 pounds beef liver, washed and drained
2 large onions, chopped
1 teaspoon pepper
1 teaspoon turmeric
¼ cup lemon juice
2 cups water
¼ cup vegetable oil

Kurdish Beef Pocket (Borek)

First, prepare the dough by mixing the flour with yeast, water, and a pinch of salt. Slowly pour in the vegetable oil while kneading with your hands. Add a little more water to hold the dough together if needed. Cover with plastic wrap. Allow to rise for 1½ hours at room temperature.

In the meantime, prepare the filling by putting the ground beef in a skillet and let it cook in its juice for ten minutes. Add grated onions, salt and pepper; allow to cook for 10–15 minutes or until the meat is done. Set aside to cool.

Divide the dough into small golf ball–size pieces.

Note: I like to dip my hands in a bowl of water to keep the dough from sticking to my hands while stuffing the dough balls. Flatten the dough balls into thin circles and place a tablespoon of filling in the middle; close the dough to form half a circle and twist the edges to make a triangular shape. Repeat this step until all dough is finished.

Heat the vegetable oil in a pan. Slowly drop the *borek* in hot oil and fry both sides until golden. Borek is a great appetizer, and it can be served as a main meal with salad.

Note: You can also use any kind of spring/egg roll pastry dough. Follow the package directions for thawing.

Dough
3 cups flour
1 cup vegetable oil
1 teaspoon yeast
½ cup water (more if needed to prepare the dough)
Salt

Filling
1 pound lean ground beef
1 large onion, grated
1 teaspoon ground cumin
Salt and pepper to taste
Vegetable oil for frying

Rice Kubba (Kubba Halab)

Wash rice, add salt and turmeric, and bring to a boil; reduce heat to low. Allow to cook until rice is soft, but not too mushy, and definitely not crunchy. Remove the rice from the pot and into a large bowl. Allow to cool completely.

In the same pot, brown the meat; add chopped onions, parsley, almonds, salt and pepper, and cumin; mix cooked until the liquid has evaporated. Add raisins and mix again. Set aside at a room temperature to cool off.

Place the cooked rice in a food processor and mix well (or mix by hand until dough is smooth). You may have to add a bit of water as you mix.

To form the kubba, have a bowl of water near you to wet your hands with so the dough does not stick to your hands. Take a walnut-sized ball of dough, and cradling it in the palm of one hand, use your index finger of the other hand to form a hollow in the middle of the dough/ball. Fill each one with a tablespoon of the filling, seal, and pat until you form into an egg shape. Repeat this process until all the meat and rice is finished. Place onto a baking tray. Brush each with egg wash.

Heat cooking oil until sizzling hot. Drop the kubbas in the hot oil; gently swirl the pan to allow the kubba to turn themselves over as they might break because the crust is fragile.

Fry both sides until golden brown. Remove and place them on a paper towel to absorb the excess oil and serve warm with torshi or any kind of salads or soups.

Kubba are mostly consumed in Iraq and Syria The name Halab is an ancient city in Syria.

Crust

2 cup rice
1½ cup water
½ teaspoon turmeric
Salt to taste

Filling

1 pound lean ground beef
1 medium onion, finely chopped
1 bunch parsley, washed and chopped
1 teaspoon cumin
1 cup chopped almonds or pine nuts (optional)
1 cup yellow raisins (optional)
2 beaten eggs for the end to brush on the kubba
for a golden color

Kubba Bulgur

Rinse the bulgur in several changes of water; let soak in fresh water for 15–20 minutes.

Put a small frying pan over medium heat and add the meat. Cook until brown. Add onion, salt, pepper, allspice, and cumin; mix well and allow to cook on low heat.

Toast the pine nuts in the dry pan until golden and fragrant. Add the roasted pine nuts to the meat mixture, taste, adjust seasoning as needed. Remove from heat and allow to cool off.

Drain the bulgur in a colander; to remove excess water, press down by squeezing in handfuls. Pour the bulgur in a large bowl. Add onions to the bulgur; add meat, allspice, cumin, and one egg. Knead by hand until the mixture comes together and all the ingredients are evenly distributed. Refrigerate for about 15–20 minutes to let the mixture chill through. (The filling process is same as making Kubba Halab).

To form the kubba, have a bowl of water near you to wet your hands with so the dough does not stick to your hands. Take a walnut-sized ball of dough, and cradling it in the palm of one hand, use your index finger of the other hand to form a hollow in the middle of the dough/ball. Fill each one with a tablespoon of the filling, and seal, eventually forming an egg shape. Drizzle with olive oil. Place the kubba on a greased baking tray. Preheat oven to 200. Bake the kubba until golden on both sides evenly. You can also fry the kubbas in oil if you prefer.

Once both sides are golden, remove from oven and drizzle a bit more olive oil. Serve with tzatziki sauce or salad.

Crust

1 cup fine bulgur (fine cracked wheat)
1 pound lean ground beef or lamb
1 teaspoon ground allspice
1 egg
Salt and pepper to taste

Filling

1 pound lean ground beef
2 medium onion, finely grated
1 teaspoon allspice
1 teaspoon cumin
1 cup chopped almonds or pine nuts (optional)
1 cup vegetable oil (if frying instead of baking)
Olive oil

Vegetable Samosa

In a deep nonstick pan, sauté all the vegetables over medium-high heat; cook until all the vegetables are tender and cooked through. Add curry, salt and pepper. Mix well and sauté for another 10 minutes. Remove from heat and allow to cool to room temperature.

Set the egg roll pastry strips in front of you. Place a teaspoon of the vegetable filling in the center of one end of the pastry dough. Fold over the corner to the edge to enclose the filling; continue folding pastry to a triangle shape. Seal with egg wash to prevent from opening. Set aside on a tray until all samosa are done.

Heat oil in a frying pan until sizzling hot. Add the samosa one at a time into the oil. Fry until golden on both sides. Place a paper towel on a platter. Add the samosas to the platter. You can serve as a main dish with salad or soup or as an appetizer.

Note: This is a great party dish.

1 package egg roll pastry dough
1 large potato, peeled and chopped
1 cup frozen peas
2 medium carrots, finely chopped
2 medium onions, finely chopped
1 tablespoon curry powder
2 egg yolks
Enough vegetable oil for frying

Kurdish Beef Egg Roll

skillet on medium-high heat; drain any excess liquid. Add onions, allspice, salt and pepper; mix well. Cook for 10 minutes or until onions are translucent. Pour the mixture into a bowl and let it cool at room temperature. Once the mixture has cooled off, prepare the egg rolls by laying one wrapper on a clean cutting board and placing 1 tablespoon of the beef filling onto the center and roll up. Roll until all edges are sealed (similar to Chinese egg rolls). Before you seal, brush the edges with the egg wash to prevent from opening.

In a medium saucepan, heat oil until its sizzling hot. Slowly drop in one egg roll at a time to deep-fry for 2–3 minutes on each side. Remove the egg roll from the oil. Place a paper towel on a plate and put the fried egg rolls on the paper towel to absorb any excess oil. Continue frying the egg rolls until all done and serve hot with a side dish of your choice.

1 pound lean ground beef
1 medium onion, chopped
1 tablespoon allspice
1 package wonton wrappers
1 beaten egg mixed with 1 tablespoon water
Enough oil to deep fry
Brown the beef in a large nonstick

Roasted Stuffed Chicken

Wash and rinse rice and put it in a pot, then add 1 cup hot water, one tablespoon oil, and a pinch of salt. Cover and bring to a boil. Reduce heat to low and let it simmer for 10 minutes until al dente.

In a frying pan, heat some oil and add almonds and cook until brown. Remove from heat and mix in the raisins until they are puffy. Remove the almonds and the raisins from the pan and set aside.

Wash and rinse the chicken inside out and rub inside and out with lemon juice. Season the chicken with nutmeg, allspice, salt and pepper inside and out; place in a Pyrex baking dish.

Mix the cooked rice with the raisin/almond mixture. This is your stuffing. Take enough of the stuffing to place inside the chicken cavity until it's full.

Cover the chicken with aluminum foil and bake for 45 minutes at 350 degrees. To get the top golden and crispy, broil on low for 15 minutes. Remove the foil and poke the chicken with toothpicks, pouring the juice from the chicken back over the top. Transfer the chicken to a platter and serve with salad of your choice.

1 whole chicken (any size you desire)
1 cup uncooked long-grain basmati rice
1 cup roasted almonds, chopped
1 cup yellow raisins
¼ cup lemon juice (or two fresh lemons)
1 teaspoon nutmeg
1 teaspoon allspice
½ cup olive oil
Salt and pepper to taste

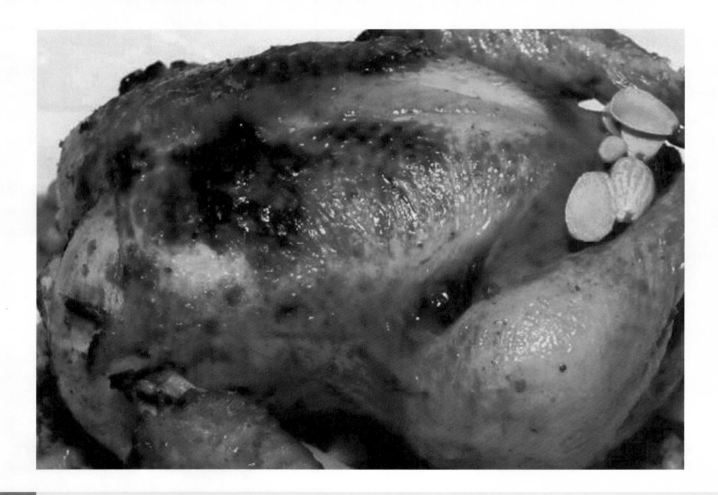

Stuffed Potato with Cheddar

Preheat the oven to 350 degrees. Lightly grease a large baking pan. Wash the potatoes, then pierce each one with the tip of a knife or fork and put them in a pot of boiling water. Let them cook on high for 10 minutes or until they are soft.

Remove the potatoes from the water and cut them vertically in half. Scoop out the inside of each potato and discard. Deep-fry the potato in hot oil until golden, then remove and drain on a paper towel to absorb the excess oil. Lay the potatoes on the baking pan and fill each potato with cheese. Bake in the oven for 10 minutes or until the cheese is completely melted. Top with sour cream and a sprinkling of chives.

6 large potatoes, scrubbed clean
1 cup shredded cheddar cheese
1 bunch fresh chives, chopped
1 cup vegetable oil
1 cup sour cream
Water
Salt and pepper to taste

Stuffed Biscuits with Spinach

In a pan, heat some oil and sauté the onions until translucent. Next, add spinach and sauté for 5 minutes. Add shredded cheddar cheese and cook until melted.

In the meantime, cut the biscuits in half (two pieces), forming a top and bottom. Press bottom half of the biscuit into a lightly greased baking pan, and then put a tablespoon of the mixture in the center of the cut biscuit. Put the other half of the biscuit on top of the other. Press the edges together, ensuring to lock in the mixture. Repeat this process until all biscuits are complete; lay the biscuits about 1 inch apart. Brush each biscuit with the beaten egg. Bake at 350 degrees for 10 minutes.

1 can Pillsbury buttermilk biscuits
1 bunch fresh spinach, washed and chopped (or 1 small bag frozen spinach, thawed)
1 medium onion, finely chopped
1 bunch parsley, washed and finely chopped
1 cup shredded cheddar cheese
1 egg, beaten
¼ cup oil
Salt and pepper to taste

This dish makes a great appetizer or breakfast meal.

Feta Cheese and Mushroom Hot Pocket

In a pan, melt butter over medium heat. Add onions and sauté until translucent. Next, add mushrooms and one egg into the mixture. Stir until the mushrooms are tenderized. Add cheese, salt and pepper, immediately remove from the stove and allow to cool at room temperature.

Cut the biscuits in half (two pieces), forming a top and bottom. Press bottom half of the biscuit into a lightly greased baking pan, and then put a tablespoon of the mixture in the center of the cut biscuit. Put the other half of the biscuit on top of the other. Press the edges together, ensuring to lock in the mixture. Repeat this process until all biscuits are complete; lay the biscuits about one inch apart. Brush each biscuit with the beaten egg. Bake at 350 degrees for 10 minutes.

1 can Pillsbury buttermilk biscuits
1 pound mushroom, chopped
1 medium onion, finely chopped
1 cup feta cheese
1 stick butter
1 large egg
1 egg yolk to brush the top
Salt and pepper to taste

This makes a great breakfast meal.

Garlic Pasta

Cook egg noodles according to the directions on the package. Drain and set aside. In a large skillet, melt butter and sauté garlic for 2 minutes. Add the cooked noodles, salt and pepper; mix well. Reduce the heat to low, cover and cook for 5 more minutes. Add the parsley and mix well. Transfer to a plate and sprinkle with Parmesan cheese. Serve with toss salad.

Note: I usually create or come up with a quick entrée like this when I do not have time to cook traditional Kurdish food.

1 pound uncooked egg noodles
1 bunch fresh parsley, chopped
1 cup grated Parmesan cheese
5 garlic cloves, minced
½ cup butter
Water
Salt and pepper to taste

Spaghetti

In a pan, cook the ground beef until the meat is browned on medium-high heat. Add onions and cook until transparent. Mix in the ginger, garlic, carrots, and mushrooms. Let this mixture cook for 5 minutes or until the carrots are softened. Add crushed tomatoes and the tomato paste into the meat mixture. Add 2 cups water and the olive oil minus 1 tablespoon (reserve for cooking the pasta) into the mixture. Let the mixture cook on low heat until the sauce thickens.

Cook the pasta in water, including salt and olive oil. Once cooked, drain it and add to the meat sauce. Once combined, heat the sauce and pasta for approximately 15 minutes, covered.

Serve with garlic bread and salad.

1 package spaghetti noodles
1 pound ground beef
1 large onion, chopped
1 cup mushrooms, chopped
1 cup carrots, chopped
1 (10 oz.) can crushed tomatoes
1 (6 oz.) can tomato paste
4 cloves of garlic, chopped
½ teaspoon fresh ginger, chopped
¼ cup olive oil
Water
Salt and pepper to taste

Salad Olivieh (Persian Style)

In a large bowl, combine the chicken with the eggs, pickles, potatoes, celery and mix well.

In a separate bowl, mix together mayonnaise, Dijon mustard, lemon juice, oil, turmeric, salt and pepper. Pour this dressing over the chicken mixture. Cover and place in fridge for a few hours, allowing the flavors to come together. Pour the salad mix on a platter. Garnish with olives and pickles, shredded carrots, or anything you like.

Note: I credit this recipe to my sister. This dish is a popular Iranian recipe.

1 pound cooked chicken breast, shredded
4 large potatoes, boiled and cut in small cubes
4 hard-boiled eggs, cut in small cubes
2 sticks celery, finely chopped
2 cups dill pickles, finely chopped
½ cup frozen peas (washed and rinsed)
½ cup frozen carrots (washed and rinsed)
3 teaspoons lime juice
2 cups mayonnaise
2 teaspoons Dijon mustard
 cup olive oil
1 teaspoon turmeric
3 cups water
Salt and white ground pepper to taste

Kurdish Grilled Chicken Salad

Preheat the grill to medium heat. In a large bowl, pour in the oil and the vinegar. Whisk until well combined. Add the oregano, garlic, salt and pepper to your taste. Wash and rinse the chicken, and then coat it with cooking spray. Sprinkle the chicken with salt and pepper; toss the chicken on the grill until golden brown on both sides. While grilling, slice chicken diagonally with knife and fork, but be careful not to burn your hands. Immediately, transfer the grilled chicken into a bowl and apply half of the vinegar dressing over the meat. Cool for five minutes. Remove the chicken from the mixture and put onto a plate.

Combine the cucumbers, tomatoes, onions, lettuce, olives, and feta into a glass bowl and toss. Next, add the remaining vinegar dressing over the salad. Mix well. Transfer the salad onto a plate and toss with the sliced chicken.

Note: This recipe was shared by my brother. This makes a great summer meal.

5 boneless, skinless chicken breasts
6 cups romaine lettuce, torn into bite-size pieces
6 lemon wedges
3 tablespoons red wine vinegar
2 cucumbers, sliced thinly
2 tablespoons fresh oregano, chopped
1 clove garlic, minced
1 cup grape tomatoes, halved lengthwise
1 cup feta cheese
¼ cup extra-virgin olive oil
¼ cup pitted green olives, halved lengthwise
¼ small red onion, sliced lengthwise
Salt and pepper to taste

KURDISH SIDE
Salads

Kurdish Salad

Wash and dice the cucumbers to ½-inch thickness and toss it in a bowl. Add the red onion, tomatoes, and dry mint; mix well. Top with dressing below.

6 Persian cucumbers (or 2 seedless English cucumbers)
5 red round tomatoes, diced
1 medium red onion, chopped
2 tablespoon dry mint
½ cup fresh lime or lemon juice
Salt and pepper to taste

In a medium bowl, whisk the olive oil, lemon juice, garlic, salt and pepper. Stir just before serving over the salad.

Dressing
2 cloves garlic, minced
½ cup fresh lemon juice
¼ cup extra-virgin olive oil
Salt and pepper to taste

Yogurt and Cucumber Sauce

Yogurt sauce is very common throughout the Middle East, although each country has a unique name. The Greeks call is *tzatziki*, Kurds call it *khiyar mast* and the Turks call is *cacik*. We, Kurds, also eat plain yogurt for breakfast and make cold refreshing drinks *douh* or *doogh*.

Mix the grated cucumber, minced garlic, dill, and salt and set aside for 10 minutes. Stir in the yogurt and beat with a fork until the mixture is smooth, then add olive oil and salt; stir again until the consistency of a thick soup. Refrigerate for 1 hour and serve cold.

2 cups plain yogurt (homemade or store bought)
3 seeded medium cucumbers, peeled and grated
3 garlic cloves, peeled and finely minced
1 tablespoon dry dill (you can also use fresh if you like)
1 tablespoon dried mint
1 tablespoon extra-virgin olive oil
Salt to taste

Purslane and Yogurt Salad (Pirpêne)

Gently nip off the tender and leafy portions of purslane. Bring a pot of water to a boil; add the purslane. Boil for 3–4 minutes. Drain and rinse with cold water; set aside.

In a deep bowl, add the garlic with a pinch of salt and combine until it becomes a thick paste. Add yogurt and mix it thoroughly. Add a dash of water to loosen the yogurt if it's too thick. Squeeze excess water from the purslane and place the purslane leaves in the yogurt mix. *Gently* mix together. Sprinkle a little cayenne pepper and drizzle olive oil over the yogurt mixture. Ready to serve.

Note: This is a very simple, refreshing, and delicious salad. You can find purslane in most Middle Eastern or Asian grocery stores. This can also be used as a dip.

1 bunch purslane (a succulent herb), chopped
1 clove garlic, minced
1 cup Greek yogurt
1 tablespoon olive oil
1 teaspoon cayenne pepper (optional)
Water for boiling

Yogurt and Shallot Dip (Mast o Musir)

Mix yogurt and diced shallots in a bowl. Add salt and pepper to taste. Cover the mixture and allow to settle for about one hour in the refrigerator.

Serve this as a side to any main dish or use it as a dip with chips or bread.

3 cups plain yogurt (prefer homemade or Greek yogurt)
2 shallots, diced
Salt and pepper to taste

Cilantro Sauce

Remove the seeds from the chilies and chop. Mix the cilantro, green chilies, lemon juice, and garlic together thoroughly in a small bowl. Slowly add sugar and salt; mix well.

Pour the sauce into a glass jar, screw on the lid, and store in the refrigerator for one week before serving.

Note: An Afghani friend gave me this recipe. This sauce is very good as a dip or with a kabob dish.

2 bunches fresh cilantro, minced
2 hot green chilies
4 cloves garlic, minced
1 tablespoon sugar
1 cup lemon juice
Salt to taste

Kurdish Pickled Vegetables (Torshi)

In a large bowl, add turnips and 1 teaspoon of salt. Mix well and set aside. In another large bowl, add carrots, celery, cauliflower, remaining salt, turmeric, and all other spices. Mix together well. Set aside for 30 minutes. Scoop out the turnips from the bowl and add to the other vegetables. Mix well until all vegetables are well coated with the spices.

Take the vegetables and put into a large glass jar. Pour the vinegar over the vegetables in the jar; it should go about an inch above the vegetables. Add any additional salt (as desired). Seal the jar. Store in a cool place for one week before opening the jar.

After a week, open the jar and taste; add more salt if needed. If it's too sour, take 2 tablespoons molasses or honey to neutralize. Close and store in a cool place for an additional week. Open and taste it again after a week. Adjust the salt/spice to your preference. The vegetables should have a pickled taste.

Note: This is ready after 3–4 weeks. It's a pickled dish that is served with kabobs, sandwiches, or rice dishes. Always keep it stored in a cool place, such as the fridge.

5 turnips, washed and peeled, cut in cubes
5 large carrots, washed and peeled, cut in cubes (or use baby carrots)
1 bunch celery, chopped
1 medium head cauliflower
1 head garlic (peeled and leave as a whole)
¼ cup dried mint
½ cup dried tarragon
4 teaspoons turmeric
3 teaspoons coarse salt (or more depending on preference)
2 teaspoons curry powder
½ gallon white or cider vinegar
30-ounce glass jar (or larger)

KURDISH
Sweets

Baklava

Prepare the syrup first. Boil the water, add sugar, and mix until dissolved. Add cardamom, cinnamon, saffron, and lemon juice to the sugar water. Bring the mixture to a boil on medium heat. Boil for about 45 minutes to 1 hour until it becomes syrupy. Set it aside for cooling.

In a large bowl, prepare filling mixture. Combine walnuts, cardamom, cinnamon, and sugar. Add half stick of melted butter, mix well, and then set aside.

Spread one sheet of phyllo dough on a large well-greased cookie sheet. Brush the entire surface with melted butter. Continue layering the phyllo sheets and brushing using half the box of phyllo (about 8 sheets). Spread the filling mixture evenly over the pastry dough. Layer the rest of the phyllo sheets on top of the mixture, one at a time, and coating each sheet with butter before layering the next.

Preheat oven to 350 degrees. Cut into squares or diamond shape. Bake for 20–30 minutes, removing when golden brown. Immediately drizzle the syrup evenly over the top. Run a knife through the previously cut grooves.

Sprinkle with pistachios. Allow to cool for 1 hour before serving.

Note: Baklava syrup is normally not made this way, but I prefer these ingredients instead of including rose water, which is normally used to make the syrup. Try this, you'll love it!

1 box phyllo pastry at room temperature for 1–2 hours
3 sticks melted butter for brushing phyllo dough

Filling
3½ cups walnuts, finely chopped
2 tablespoons ground cardamom
½ stick melted butter
1 tablespoon ground cinnamon
½ cup of sugar (or sugar substitute)

Syrup
5 saffron threads, dissolved in ½ cup hot water
2 tablespoons lemon juice
2 cups sugar
1 cup water
1 teaspoon cardamom
1 teaspoon cinnamon
½ cup chopped pistachios (for garnish)

Ladyfinger Baklava

Prepare the syrup first. Boil the water, add sugar, and mix until dissolved. Add rose or orange blossom water and lemon juice. Bring the mixture to a boil on medium heat. Boil for about 45 minutes to 1 hour until it becomes syrupy. Set it aside for cooling.

In a large bowl, prepare the filling mixture. Combine walnuts, sugar, rose water, or orange blossom and the egg white. Mix well until the walnut and the sugar are well combined.

Place one sheet of phyllo dough on a clean work surface and brush with melted butter; continue this step until you reach the fourth sheet of the dough. Place a 1 tablespoon of the filling on the edge of the pastry; start to roll halfway up; cut in half. Put the roll on a well-greased baking tray. Start using the other half of four layers by filling it with the walnut filling and roll and put it next to the other roll on the baking tray. Repeat the above step until all dough is gone.

Preheat oven to 350 degrees. Brush with melted butter and cut each one into 3–4 pieces and bake for 25 minutes or until the crust becomes golden. Remove from the oven and immediately drizzle the syrup over the ladyfinger baklava. Run a knife through the previously cut grooves and garnish each one with crushed pistachio (optional).

Filling
1 box phyllo pastry at room temperature for 1–2 hours
3 sticks melted butter for brushing phyllo dough
1½ cup walnuts, finely chopped
1 teaspoon rose water or orange blossom water (use one or the other, but not both)
1 sticks unsalted butter, melted
2 teaspoons sugar
1 egg white only

Syrup
2 cups sugar
1 cup water
2 tablespoons lemon juice
1 teaspoon rose water or orange blossom water
½ cup pistachios, chopped (for garnish)

Sweet Cheese Kunafa

To make the syrup, bring 2 cups water to boil and add sugar; mix until sugar is dissolved. Add orange blossom and cardamom. Bring the mixture to a boil on medium heat. Boil for about 45 minutes to an hour until it becomes syrupy, and then set it aside for cooling.

Remove the kataif from the package and start by shredding with your hands into small pieces. Melt half a stick of the sweet butter. Add to the kataif and mix well by hand until all pieces are coated. You don't want it to be soggy.

Take the kataif mixture and place in a large nonstick pan/wok; roast in the same butter that it's already been coated in over medium heat. Do not add any more butter. Cook until golden and crispy. Remove from heat.

In a round glass Pyrex dish, coat well with saffron butter. Divide the kataif mixture into two portions. Take half the kataif and add to the Pyrex dish and pat down. Add the mozzarella cheese on top and pat down. Add the remaining kataif on top of the cheese and pat down.

Preheat oven to 350 degrees. Bake kunafa in the oven for about 10–15 minutes or until the dough is evenly golden brown. Once the kunafa is done, remove from oven. Drizzle with the warm syrup when ready to serve.

Note: This dish can be made ahead of time and placed in the fridge without the syrup. Before serving, warm up the syrup to lukewarm and drizzle over. Cut into a pie shape.

Dessert
1 package kataif shredded pastry dough (check your local Mediterranean groceries); similar to vermicelli
2 sticks unsalted sweet butter
1 tablespoon orange blossom water
2 cups finely shredded mozzarella
½ teaspoon saffron, dissolved in 1 teaspoon melted butter

Syrup
2 cups water
1 cup sugar
1 tablespoon orange blossom (or rose water if you prefer)
1 teaspoon crushed cardamom

Zolobia

Place yogurt and cornstarch in a mixing bowl; mix well. Let sit for 5 minutes. Add flour, 2 tablespoons rose water, butter, baking soda, and dissolved saffron. Beat with a mixer until the batter is smooth (I use a hand mixer). Let it stand for 30 minutes.

Meanwhile make the syrup in a deep saucepan (enough for dipping zolobias). Combine water and sugar in a small saucepan. Bring to a boil over medium-high heat. Continue heating until sugar is completely dissolved and the syrup thickens, stirring occasionally. Add lemon; mix well. Turn off the heat, but leave syrup on stove.

Transfer the batter to an empty ketchup bottle or similar bottle with a skinny tip. You can also use a ziplock bag, snipping off a corner to make a ¼-inch-wide hole (you can use a funnel instead of ziplock).

In a deep medium skillet, heat the oil over medium-high heat. Reduce the heat to medium. Squeeze out the batter about 3–4 times in a circular motion into hot oil. Be careful, the oil may splash! Fry until golden brown on both sides, turning once. Add more oil if necessary.

Using tongs or flat spatula, carefully remove zolobia from the oil. Drop gently into syrup. Let it stand in syrup for a few minutes while you fry the others. Place them in a colander (do not place the zolobias on top of each other while draining, just a single layer, otherwise they will get soggy).

Then transfer the zolobia to plate. Refrigerate before serving.

Note: This is a great dessert with tea or coffee.

1 cup plain yogurt
¼ cup flour
2 cups cornstarch
2 tablespoons rose water (You can find it at any Middle Eastern grocery.)
½ teaspoon saffron, dissolved in 1 tablespoon hot water
1 tablespoon butter, softened at room temperature
½ teaspoon baking soda
Canola oil (or any liquid cooking oil for frying)

Luqm Qazi

In a bowl, combine both flours, yogurt, yeast, and the sugar; mix well. Slowly pour in water and mix by hand to form a dough. Make sure you don't leave any lumps (the dough should not be thick or watery; it should have a muddy consistency). Cover the bowl with saran wrap and leave at room temperature to allow the dough to rise for two hours.

To make the syrup, combine water and sugar in a small saucepan. Bring to boil and cook until the sugar has dissolved; gradually mix. Add cardamom, saffron, and lemon juice; continue boiling until the syrup has thickened. Remove from heat and allow to cool.

After two hours when the dough rises, you are ready to fry the *luqm*. Heat oil until sizzling hot in a deep nonstick pan. Take a teaspoon of the dough and slowly drop into the hot oil; you can fry several at the same time. Deep fry until golden brown.

Place a paper towel onto a plate and remove the fried luqm from the oil; add to the plate. The paper towel will absorb excess oil. Once all have been fried, transfer the luqm to a large bowl and pour the syrup over them. Make sure to coat them all. Using a spatula, mix slowly. Ready to serve.

Note: This dish is traditionally made during the month of Ramadan (the Muslim holy month) and is served with tea as a dessert.

1 cup white flour
1 teaspoon corn flour
2 tablespoon yogurt
1 teaspoon dry yeast
1 teaspoon sugar
½ cup warm water

Syrup
1 cup sugar
1 teaspoon cardamom powder
½ teaspoon saffron (optional)
1 teaspoon lemon juice
1¼ cup water

2 cups vegetable oil for frying

Kolicha with Walnuts

Pour 1 packet of yeast in ½ cup hot water in a large cup. Mix and set aside for 10 minutes. After 10 minutes, mix the flour, butter, salt, and the yeast mixture in a large bowl with a spoon. Slowly incorporate the olive oil and mix by hand until a smooth, nonsticky dough is achieved (like cookie dough). Cover the dough with a towel or a saran wrap and set aside. Now you're ready to make the filling.

In a bowl, pour walnuts, coconut, sugar, cardamom, nutmeg, and the butter; mix well. Now you're ready to assemble.

Assembly: Spray some oil or Pam on a baking tray to keep them from sticking. Portion out the dough into golf ball–size pieces. Fill each circle of the dough with the walnut mixture; fold the circle over to create a half circle and tuck the edges to seal and place them on the tray. Brush the surface of all cookies with the egg yolk. Poke the top of each cookie with a fork to make 4 holes on top (to decorate).

Preheat oven to 350 degrees. Bake the cookies for about 20–30 minutes or until golden. Take them out and allow to cool before serving.

Note: Kulichas were traditionally made for large celebrations, Kurdish New Year *(Newroz)* and special occasions. Today, since most ingredients are readily available, they are made anytime. To store kulichas, place them in an airtight container. They can last up to one month in the fridge.

Dough

3 cups white all-purpose flour

1 pack dry yeast (dissolved in warm water for 10 minutes)

2 sticks of butter (soften at room temperature)

1 teaspoon salt

½ cup olive oil (If you need the dough to be softer, then use this; otherwise just use it on your hand to keep the dough from sticking.)

Filling

2 cups chopped walnuts

2 cups shredded coconut (optional)

½ cup white sugar

½ stick of butter (at room temperature)

1 teaspoon ground cardamom (optional)

¼ teaspoon ground nutmeg (optional)

2 egg yolk, beaten (to brush on before baking)

Kolicha with Dates

Pour 1 packet of yeast in ½ cup hot water in a large cup. Mix and set aside for 10 minutes. After 10 minutes, mix the flour, butter, salt, and the yeast mixture in a large bowl with a spoon. Slowly incorporate the olive oil and mix by hand until a smooth, nonsticky dough is achieved (like cookie dough). Cover the dough with a towel or a saran wrap and set aside. Now you're ready to make the filling.

Place the dates in a large bowl, add coconut (optional), sugar, cardamom, and butter; mix well until smooth. Now you're ready to make the *kulicha*.

Assembly: Two ways to make the kulicha dates. One is same as the walnut kulicha—portion out the dough into golf ball–size pieces.

The second method is to divide the dough and filling into 3–4 portions. Take each portion of the dough and flatten with a dough roller. Place a large piece of saran wrap on a table and add the date mixture on top of it. Place another piece of saran wrap over top of the mixture. This will prevent the dates from sticking to your rolling pin. Roll the saran wrap to flatten the date mixture. It should be the same thickness as your dough that you previously flattened. Remove the top portion of the saran wrap. Lift the date mixture with the bottom saran wrap. Flip the date on top of the portioned dough. Repeat this with the remaining date and dough portions.

Spread the filling mixture evenly over the pastry dough and roll it up and cut into small pieces. Brush the surface of all cookies with egg yolk for golden color. Preheat oven to 350 degrees. Bake for about 20 minutes or until golden. Take them out and allow to cool. Ready to serve when cooled.

Note: To store kulichas, place them in an airtight container. They can last up to one month in the fridge.

Dough

3 cups white all-purpose flour

1 pack dry yeast (dissolved in warm water for 10 minutes)

2 sticks of butter (soften at room temperature)

1 teaspoon salt

½ cup olive oil (If you need the dough to be softer, then use this; otherwise just use it on your hand to keep the dough from sticking.)

Filling

2½ cup baking dates, pitted and softened at room temperature

½ stick butter, melted

1 tablespoon ground cardamom (optional)

2 cups coconuts, shredded (optional)

2 egg yolk, beaten (to brush on before baking)

Mahalabia

In a nonstick pot, boil 2 cups milk and the sugar over medium heat. In the meantime, mix the cornstarch with remaining 1 cup cold milk until smooth and set aside.

When the milk and sugar mixture has thickened, turn off heat but keep it on the stove. Add to this, the cold milk and cornstarch mixture, rose water, and crushed cardamom; mix well. Pour in a glass plate (you can pour into individual ice-cream serving cups if you prefer) and allow to cool for 3–4 hours in the refrigerator.

3 cups whole milk
3 cups sugar
6 tablespoons cornstarch
1 cup cold water
1 tablespoon rose water
1 teaspoon crushed cardamom (optional)
1 teaspoon cinnamon
3 tablespoon crushed pistachio (roasted)

Garnish the top with pistachio, cinnamon, and if you like, add a pinch of cardamom before serving. I personally like to serve in a large bowl so everyone can scoop out as much as they want.

Note: This is a great dessert to bring to a dinner party.

Cardamom-Flavored Cookies (Shakirlama)

Preheat oven to 350 degrees. Grease baking tray.

In a large bowl, mix butter and sugar until well combined.

In a separate bowl, combine the flour, cardamom, and baking powder; mix well with a spoon or by hand to form a dough.

Pinch off a golf ball–sized piece of the dough. Roll the piece of dough in your hand; slightly press it flat on the greased baking tray; place one almond on each cookie. Bake for 20 minutes and remove from the oven. Allow to cool completely before removing them from the tray; otherwise they will break.

Note: Leave an inch between each cookie. They expand when baked and will stick together if too close.

2½ cups flour (I use all purpose flour.)
1 cup sugar
3 sticks butter (room temperature)
½ teaspoon baking powder
1 teaspoon ground cardamom
½ cup blanched almonds

Raisin Cookies

Combine the sugar, eggs, melted butter, and vanilla; mix well until the dough is creamy. Add currants or raisins and fold them into the flour. Preheat oven to 350 degrees.

Spread out wax paper on a cookie sheet. Take a teaspoonful of the batter and drop it on the wax paper, leaving 2 inches between each cookie. Bake 10–15 minutes or until slightly golden. Remove the cookies from the oven and allow them to cool. Gently lift the cookies off the wax paper and put them on a plate and serve with tea or coffee.

2 cups all-purpose flour

4 eggs

1 cup unsalted butter, melted

1¾ cups sugar

2 cups currants (or use raisins if you prefer)

1 teaspoon vanilla extract

Almond Brittle (No Bake)

In a medium saucepan, mix the sugar, heavy cream, butter, and corn syrup. Cook over medium heat. Stir with a wooden spoon constantly until this mixture boils. Add almonds, saffron, rose water, and salt to the mixture. Cook it on medium-high heat for about 5–7 minutes until the mixture is golden brown and thick. Once thickened, remove from heat immediately.

Line a baking sheet with parchment or wax paper. Pour the mixture onto the baking sheet immediately. With a large flat spatula, sprinkle the top with pistachios and pat them down into the thick mixture.

Allow this mixture to cool for 1 hour. Remove from parchment paper and break into pieces. Enjoy this tasty dessert.

2 tablespoons raw chopped pistachios
2 tablespoons barberries, rinsed and patted dry
2 tablespoons raw almonds
1 cup sugar
1½ teaspoon saffron
1 tablespoon rose water
½ teaspoon sea salt
¼ cup heavy cream
½ cup unsalted butter in small cubes
¼ cup light corn syrup
1 cup chopped pistachio

Saffron-Flavored Halwa

Dissolve the rice flour in water. Simmer over medium heat in a medium-sized saucepan for 5 minutes, stirring constantly to prevent sticking. Add sugar and stir until dissolved. Add saffron and mix well. Mix in the butter, stir, and let simmer for 5 more minutes until the consistency is like pudding.

Pour onto a flat dinner plate and garnish with pistachio or almonds or both.

Note: Halwa can be served hot or cold and generally is served as a dessert.

½ cup rice flour
2 tablespoons butter, room temperature
1 cup water
4 tablespoons sugar
½ teaspoon saffron dissolved in 1 tablespoon hot water
Pistachio or toasted almonds to garnish

DRINKS

In Kurdistan and throughout the Middle East, there are seemingly endless varieties of drinks with the delicate essence of fruit or blossoms known as sherbet, but fruit juice, tea, and doogh are the most common drink.

Chai/Chay

Chay means tea in Kurdish. Kurds commonly serve chay at breakfast, after lunch and dinner, or for midday break. By far, the most common drink among Kurds and the rest of the Middle East is tea. In Kurdistan, tea is usually served in small transparent glasses with sugar or sipped with cubes of sugar. When guests visit, hosts serve tea regardless of the time of day. Kurds always serve tea at religious ceremonies at mosques, at national celebrations, at times of sorrow, or during times of joy, such as weddings or picnics. We serve hot tea in the winter to keep warm or in the summer to cool off.

We believe that tea calms you down and keeps you perked up as well. Kurds drink tea more than they do coffee, so a lot of attention must go into tea preparation. Tea is always welcomed as much as a wine that is in the west.

Kurds make tea in a pot called a *samawar*. You may find samawars and *istekans* (small teacups) at any Middle Eastern grocery stores.

First, you boil water in the samawar. You take the smaller teapot that comes with the samawar, add loose black tea leaves to the small teapot; add boiled water from the larger samawar. Place the smaller teapot on the top of the samawar to simmer. The top of the samawar has holes, which releases steam to the smaller teapot, allowing the tea to steep. Often, guests drink more than one cup of tea; so for replenishment, keep boiled water ready. Pour a small amount of the tea from the smaller teapot and then pour water from the samawar, considering one's taste and desired tea color (light or dark). Kurds use the words *kem rang* for light color, which is not very strong, and *tari* for a darker-colored or stronger tea.

Note: If you do not have a samawar, you can get one large kettle and one small teapot that will sit on top of the larger kettle (with its lid removed) to simmer.

Yogurt Drink (Mast Av or Doogh)

Place yogurt in small pitcher or large glass and beat well. Add the cold water/soda, crushed mint, salt and stir well. Serve over ice. Makes 1–2 servings

Note: This is a very popular drink among the Kurds for most meals except breakfast. It's very refreshing and healthy. I prefer club soda in this because of the carbonation.qe

1½ cups cold water or club soda
1 cup yogurt
½ teaspoon crushed mint
Ice (optional)
Salt to taste

General Index*

A

Abu Ghraib, 34
Akrawi families, 19
Al-Anfal Campaign, 29
Algiers Agreement, 23–24, 29
Aqrah, 11–12, 15, 17–19, 26, 31–32
Arabs, 20, 29
Arba'illu, 20
Ataturk, Kemal, 13

B

Ba'ath Party, 15, 17, 20–21
Baghdad, 9, 20, 33–34
bakeries, 38
Bakir, Ahmed Hassan al-, 17
Baniya, 35
Barzan, 11, 13–14, 16–21, 23–24
Barzani, Ahmed, 16–17, 19
Barzani, Masoud, 16
Barzani, Mohammad, 16
Barzani, Mustafa, 13–14, 16, 19–21, 23–24
Barzinji, Mahmud, 13
Bilays, 19–20
Bileh, 19–20
"Bo Kê Bikim Gazî û Hawar," 29
bombings, 7, 19–20
borek, 83
Brigade Special Troops Battalion, 9
bulgur, 52, 85
Bush , George H. W., 29
Bush, George W., 32

C

cacik, 96
camps, 24–26
Catholic Charities, 28
chay, 114

U

United States, 9, 23–25, 27–29, 32, 37
United States Citizenship and Immigration Services, 28
uprisings, 13, 29
Urmia, 24

V

Voice of Kurdistan, 23, 26

W

Washington, DC, 24, 30–31
wife, 25
women, 7–10, 19–20, 25–26, 29

Y

Yazd, 26–27
Yezidism, 12

Z

Zebari, Chiman, 8–9, 11
  daughter, 28, 31–32
  family, 15, 17–20, 24–25, 27–28, 30
  father, 16–18, 21, 24, 29–30
  grandfather, 15, 17–18, 21
  grandmother, 15, 17–18
  husband, 25–26, 28, 31
  job, 28, 30, 32
  mother, 18, 20–21, 23, 26, 29, 31
Zebari, Hoshyar, 16
Zebari, Mahmud Agha, 16
Zebaris, 9, 16–19, 26
Zionism, 20
Zoroastrianism, 12

Kurdish Food Index*

References

Ahmetbeyzade, C. 2000. "Kurdish Nationalism in Turkey and the Role of Peasant Kurdish

    Women." In *Gender Ironies of Nationalism: Sexing the Nation*, ed. T. Mayer. New York, NY: Routledge.

Alnasrawi, A. 1994. *The Economy of Iraq: Oil, Wars, Destruction of Development and Prospects*, 1950–2010. Washington, DC: Library of Congress.

Barzani, A. 2008. "Kurdistan Is a Model for Iraq." *The Wall Street Journal*. http://online.wsj.com/news/articles/SB122645258001119425.

Barzani, A. 2008. "Sheikh Ahmed Barzani V (1896–1969)." *Kurdish Media*. Accessed May 2014. http://www.kurdmedia.com/article.aspx?id=15082.

Bengio, O. 1998. *Saddam's Word: Political Discourse in Iraq*. New York, NY: Oxford University Press.

Bruinessen, M. Van. 1992. *Aghas, Agha, Shaikh and State: The Social and Political Structures of Kurdistan*. London, UK: Zed Books.

Brunner, B. 2007. "Kurdish History Timeline," Information Please Database. Pearson Education, Inc. Accessed December 2013. http://www.infoplease.com/spot/kurds3.html.

Coughlin, C. 2005. *Saddam: His Rise and Fall*. Washington, DC: Library of Congress.
DuBois, W. E. B. 1903. *The Souls of Black Folk*. Accessed June 2014. http://www.barbleby.com/114/1.html.

Esere, M. O., J. Yusef, and J. A. Omotosho. 2011. "Influence of Spousal Communication on

    Marital Stability: Implication for Conducive Home Environment." *Edo Journal of Counseling*, 4 (1 and 2), p. 50–61. Accessed June 2014. http://www.ajol.info/index.php/ejc/article/view/72724.

Galvin, K. M. and T. M. Emmers-Sommer. 2014. "Communication—Couple Relationships, Family Relationships." Accessed July 2014. http://family.jrank.org/pages/291/Communication.html.

Graham-Brown, S. 1999. *Sanctioning Saddam: The Politics of Intervention in Iraq*. London, UK: I. B. Tauris.

Gundi, K. 2013. "United States and the Kurds in the Post-Saddam Iraq." Accessed March 2014. http://www.kurdishaspect.com/doc011113KG.html.

Koohzad, M. 2013. "Henry Kissinger: Realpolitik and Kurdish Genocide." *The Kurdish Tribune*. Accessed February 2014. http://kurdistantribune.com/2013/henry-kissinger-realpolitik-genocide/.

Kurdish Regional Government. 2009. "About the Kurdistan Regional Government." Accessed January 2014. http://www.krg.org/a/d.aspx?a=32349&l=12&r=93&s=04020000&s=010000.

Mathew, A. 2013. "Kurdish Cuisine." Accessed May 2014. http://www.onetikk.com/blog/1820/kurdish-cuisine/.

McDowall, D. 2004. *A Modern History of the Kurds*. 3rd ed. London, UK: I. B. Tauris.
Med Library. 2013. "History of the Kurdish People." Accessed May 2014. http://medlibrary.org/medwiki/History_of_the_Kurdish_people.

Meho, L. I. 2003. "The International Journal of Kurdish Studies: A Cumulative Index, 1986–2002." *The International Journal of Kurdish Studies*, 5, p. 121–140.

Meho, L. I. 2004. *The Kurdish Question in U.S. Foreign Policy: A Documentary Source*, Westport, UK: Praeger.

Metz, H. C. 2004. *Iraq: A Country Study*. Whitefish, MT: Kessinger Publishing.
Mihri, N. and N. Çakir. "Kurdish Families—Kurdish Marriage Patterns: Gender, Family, History, Family, and Marriages." *JRank Articles*. Accessed June 2014 http://family.jrank.org/pages/1026/Kurdish-Families-Kurdish-Marriage-Patterns.html#ixzz2uxePVwBr.

Nezan, Kendal. "A Brief Survey of the History of the Kurds." Accessed February 2014. http://www.institutkurde.org/en/institute/who_are_the_kurds.php.

Norwegian Refugee Council. 2010. "Iraq: Little New Displacement but Around 2.8 Million Iraqis Remain Internally Displaced." Accessed February 2014. http://www.internaldisplacement.org/assets/library/Middle-East/Iraq/pdf/Iraq-March-2010.pdf.

Schofield, R. 1989. *The Near and Middle East Titles: Iran–Iraq Border 1840–1958*. Volume 2.

Cambridge, UK: Cambridge University Press.

Selden, Z. 1999. *Economic Sanctions as Instruments of American Foreign Policy*. Washington,

DC: The Library of Congress.

"Timothy." In Bible (New International Version). 2011. https://www.bible.com/bible/111/1ti.6.10.niv

Tripp, C. 2010. *A History of Iraq*. Cambridge, UK: Cambridge University Press.
Waliy, S. 2008. "The Role and Diplomacy of Non-State Actors: Case Study on Kurds in Iraq." *Kurdish Media*. Accessed January 2014. http://kurdmedia.com/article.aspx?id=15016.

Worth, R. 2007. "Iraqi Holocaust Files." Accessed March 2014. http://iraqshoahfiles.blogspot.com.

Copyedited and indexed by Ryan Cortes

CPSIA information can be obtained at www.ICGtesting.com
Printed in the USA
LVIW01n1104090715
445596LV00004B/10